D0285615

Reconciling Rights and Responsib.....
Of Colleges and Students:
Offensive Speech, Assembly, Drug Testing, and Safety

by Annette Gibbs

ASHE-ERIC Higher Education Report No. 5, 1992

Prepared by

Clearinghouse on Higher Education
The George Washington University

In cooperation with

Association for the Study
of Higher Education

Published by

School of Education and Human Development
The George Washington University

Jonathan D. Fife, Series Editor

Cite as
Gibbs, Annette. 1992. *Reconciling Rights and Responsibilities of Colleges and Students: Offensive Speech, Assembly, Drug Testing, and Safety.* ASHE-ERIC Higher Education Report No. 5. Washington, D.C.: The George Washington University, School of Education and Human Development.

Library of Congress Catalog Card Number 92-63195
ISSN 0884-0040
ISBN 1-878380-18-4

Managing Editor: Bryan Hollister
Manuscript Editor: Barbara Fishel, Editech
Cover design by Michael David Brown, Rockville, Maryland

The ERIC Clearinghouse on Higher Education invites individuals to submit proposals for writing monographs for the *ASHE-ERIC Higher Education Report* series. Proposals must include:
1. A detailed manuscript proposal of not more than five pages.
2. A chapter-by-chapter outline.
3. A 75-word summary to be used by several review committees for the initial screening and rating of each proposal.
4. A vita and a writing sample.

ERIC **Clearinghouse on Higher Education**
School of Education and Human Development
The George Washington University
One Dupont Circle, Suite 630
Washington, DC 20036-1183

This publication was prepared partially with funding from the Office of Educational Research and Improvement, U.S. Department of Education, under contract no. ED RI-88-062014. The opinions expressed in this report do not necessarily reflect the positions or policies of OERI or the Department.

EXECUTIVE SUMMARY

Reconciling the rights and responsibilities of colleges and universities with those of their students during recent years has been problematic for numerous higher education administrators as they have sought to resolve conflicts between students and institutions. Students have charged that administrative policies and practice have directly conflicted with their constitutional rights, and administrators have responded that their responsibilities as institutional officials require them to consider the priorities of their colleges and universities in designing and implementing policy.

What Rights Do Colleges and Universities Have with Regard to Regulating Offensive Speech on Campus?

Because offensive speech is defined by its content, regulations at public colleges and universities to prohibit it raise important questions of boundaries and interpretations of the First Amendment. To date, the courts have ruled against higher education institutions' prohibiting offensive, or hate, speech because the policies failed to distinguish sanctionable speech from protected speech. In reconciling the rights of students and the responsibilities of the public institution, administrators should consider:

- Speech or expression may not be punished on the basis of the subjects the speech addresses. The government must be neutral when it regulates speech.
- Overbroad policies regulating speech have been ruled unconstitutional.
- Unduly vague policies regulating speech have been ruled unconstitutional.
- Restrictions on time, place, and manner of speech or expression appropriate for the educational environment and for maintaining order on the campus are constitutional.
- Policies based on "fighting words," even in part, cannot discriminate on the basis of content or point of view.
- Protections and procedures regarding due process should be in place before and followed during any disciplinary process.

What Issues Surround Students' Rights of Association and Assembly on Campus?

Greek social groups, gay student groups, and student religious groups continue to charge college and university administrators with denying their rights and privileges of recognition that other, less controversial groups receive. Still other students assemble on an ad hoc basis, often issue by issue, and campus demonstrations appear to have moved from protests about apartheid in South Africa to issues like abortion and AIDS. Several policy considerations seem appropriate:

- Once some student groups have been recognized, or registered, by their institution, other groups should not be denied such treatment simply because the college or university does not agree with their views.
- Student groups should be treated the same as other groups have been treated, provided they fulfill the same procedural and substantive requirements established by the institution.
- Colleges and universities are within their rights to emphasize, even through public statements, that their acknowledgment of the existence of student groups does not indicate institutional approval of the groups' or organizations' religious, political, economic, or philosophical positions.
- Student demonstrations on public college campuses, like other associational activities, cannot be prohibited on the basis of content or the message to be communicated.
- Greek groups that are primarily social in nature and also part of a national organization may be treated, as a whole, differently from other student groups in terms of institutional recognition and requirements for affiliation.
- Whatever an institution's relationship with its Greek groups, that relationship should be conveyed to all applicable groups and their respective national organizations before institutional recognition or affiliation.

What Is the Status of Mandatory Drug Testing for Athletes?

Courts in several jurisdictions have been unwilling to accept colleges' and universities' stated purposes for drug testing. Likewise, the NCAA has failed to convince most courts that it, on behalf of its member institutions, has a compelling need to test athletes randomly. While some issues surrounding testing remain debatable, the courts appear to be developing consensus about the questions and principles they will address.

- Whether an institution chooses to go along with the NCAA's testing procedures or to conduct its own testing program, it should develop clear and definitive policy objectives for its testing requirements and match those objectives to achieve the desired and stated outcome.
- The accuracy of tests is limited, and procedural safeguards should be incorporated in drug testing programs to allow students who test positive to respond to or rebut the findings. Such students could be allowed access to an additional analysis by an independent laboratory.
- The courts' most recent rulings appear to support the position that institutional *mandatory* drug testing programs violate the principle of protection of privacy guaranteed in most state constitutions.
- Strong consensus is evident among the courts that colleges and universities need to have drug education programs emphasizing prevention and rehabilitation, not only for athletes but for all students.

Finally, because an institution, if it participates in the NCAA's testing program, is the enforcer of any NCAA legislation against students, it could be subject to state laws and regulations relative to such enforcement and thus find itself between its students and the NCAA in legal claims brought by students.

What Responsibilities Do Colleges and Universities Have for Students' Safety on Campus?
In situations involving the victimization of students as well as other personal injuries to students on campus, the element of foreseeability has become a criterion in many states for determining colleges' and universities' liability. The extent to which an institution knew, or should have known, that a student was exposed, or could be exposed, to a risk of injury has become a major factor in courts' determining whether the institution owed a duty of care to the student. The courts have ruled further that:

- Institutions generally are on notice of the potential for criminal harm if similar criminal incidents have occurred in the past; harm is thus foreseeable.
- Colleges and universities should show that they exercise reasonable care to keep their campus free from conditions that create or increase the risk of harm.

- If the college or university assumes a relationship of landowner or business and invitee with its students, it may be held to similar duties of private landlords in the maintenance of physical security on the premises.
- When higher education institutions have shown that their relationships with students are not sufficiently special (landlord/tenant, for example), courts have been hesitant to impose upon them a duty to protect students from harm.
- When the college or university could not foresee harm to a student, courts have been reluctant to impose liability on the institution for the harm.

While this volume provides information necessary to the development of educational policy, it is not a substitute for the advice of legal counsel.

ADVISORY BOARD

Barbara E. Brittingham
The University of Rhode Island

Jay L. Chronister
University of Virginia

Carol Everly Floyd
Board of Regents of the Regency Universities System
State of Illinois

Rodolfo Z. Garcia
Michigan State University

Elizabeth M. Hawthorne
University of Toledo

L. Jackson Newell
University of Utah

Barbara Taylor
Association of Governing Boards of Universities and Colleges

CONSULTING EDITORS

Philip Altbach
State University of New York–Buffalo

A. Nancy Avakian
Metropolitan State University

Margaret J. Barr
Texas Christian University

Beverly Belson
Western Michigan University

Barbara B. Burn
University of Massachusetts–Amherst

L. Edwin Coate
Oregon State University

Clifton F. Conrad
University of Wisconsin–Madison

Robert Cope
Northwoods Institute

John W. Creswell
University of Nebraska–Lincoln

Dennis E. Gregory
Wake Forest University

Michael L. Hanes
West Chester University

Robert M. Hendrickson
The Pennsylvania State University

Mary Ann Heverly
Delaware County Community College

Malcolm D. Hill
The Pennsylvania State University

Edward R. Hines
Illinois State University

Clifford P. Hooker
University of Minnesota

Donald Hossler
Indiana University

Joan Isenberg
George Mason University

REVIEW PANEL

Charles Adams
University of Massachusetts–Amherst

Louis Albert
American Association for Higher Education

Richard Alfred
University of Michigan

Philip G. Altbach
State University of New York–Buffalo

Marilyn J. Amey
University of Kansas

Louis C. Attinasi, Jr.
University of Houston

Robert J. Barak
Iowa State Board of Regents

Alan Bayer
Virginia Polytechnic Institute and State University

John P. Bean
Indiana University

Louis W. Bender
Florida State University

John M. Braxton
Syracuse University

Peter McE. Buchanan
Council for Advancement and
   Support of Education

John A. Centra
Syracuse University

Arthur W. Chickering
George Mason University

Shirley M. Clark
Oregon State System of Higher Education

Darrel A. Clowes
Virginia Polytechnic Institute and State University

John W. Creswell
University of Nebraska–Lincoln

Deborah DiCroce
Piedmont Virginia Community College

Richard Duran
University of California

Kenneth C. Green
University of Southern California

Edward R. Hines
Illinois State University

Marsha W. Krotseng
West Virginia State College and University Systems

George D. Kuh
Indiana University–Bloomington

Daniel T. Layzell
Arizona Legislature

Meredith Ludwig
American Association of State Colleges and Universities

Mantha V. Mehallis
Florida Atlantic University

Robert J. Menges
Northwestern University

Toby Milton
Essex Community College

James R. Mingle
State Higher Education Executive Officers

Gary Rhoades
University of Arizona

G. Jeremiah Ryan
Harford Community College

Daryl G. Smith
Claremont Graduate School

William Tierney
Pennsylvania State University

Susan Twombly
University of Kansas

Harold Wechsler
University of Rochester

Michael J. Worth
George Washington University

CONTENTS

FOREWORD

A struggle has always been evident on college campuses between the educational mission and individual rights. Until the early 1970s, a college's relationship with its students was considered in loco parentis, or in the place of a parent. This relationship changed when all 50 states lowered the age of majority from 21 to 18, thereby granting most college students all the responsibilities, freedoms, and privileges of an adult. The one major exception was caused by the subsequent requirement for states to raise the age for drinking alcohol to 21 to be eligible for federal funding of interstate highways.

The concept of students as adults not only is central to the legal issues addressed in this report but also should be of primary consideration in reviewing all relationships between colleges and their students—present and future. Legally being an adult involves self-determination *and* self-responsibility. Fundamental to the constitutional consideration of freedom of speech and the right to associate and assemble is that adults have the right to be as unrestrained as possible in saying and meeting any other persons they want. But they are also responsible for the consequences of their actions. If by their speech or actions they break the law, they should be held accountable. Adults are held accountable only after their actions produce a legally unacceptable result—not because someone else has determined that certain speech or actions might produce an undesired result. For higher education, the dilemma is in determining where the educational process ends and the unacceptable control of an adult begins.

Another area involving the relationship between college and student considers the concept of an individual's obligation to accept the responsibility for his or her own actions and an institution's being held responsible for damaging consequences. At the heart of these considerations is who has the most control over placing or preventing the individual from being in harm's way. While students must accept the consequences of their actions as adults, institutions must not hide behind a belief that, as educational and charitable organizations, they should be less responsible than other organizations in our society with similar relationships.

This report by Annette Gibbs, professor of higher education and program director of the Center for the Study of Higher Education at the University of Virginia Curry School of Education, examines four developing areas of relationships between colleges and students: the control of offensive speech on campus, students' rights of association and assembly, mandatory drug testing for athletes, and institutions' responsibility for the safety of their students. The courts have recently considered each of these areas, which has serious consequences for the operation of higher education institutions. Dr. Gibbs examines these issues from both the viewpoint of educational mission and legality. She concludes her analysis with specific recommendations that will help institutional leaders make sounder decisions in setting policies.

Jonathan D. Fife, Series Editor,
Professor of Higher Education Administration, and
Director, ERIC Clearinghouse on Higher Education

ACKNOWLEDGMENTS

The author wishes not only to acknowledge but also to
express sincere appreciation to Paula Price for her preparation
of the manuscript with competence and cheerful participation—from first draft to final copy. Her assistance was inval-
uable. I am likewise indebted to my colleague, Jay L. Chronister, professor and chair of Educational Leadership and Policy
Studies at the Curry School, who reviewed the manuscript
and provided enthusiastic support and assistance throughout
the project. Patricia M. Lampkin, associate dean of students,
University of Virginia, was a helpful collaborator and supplied
organizational expertise during the various drafts of the
manuscript.

James J. Szablewicz, teacher and valued adviser, gave conceptual direction and technical knowledge, and I thank him
for his input. I also express my gratitude to the anonymous
reviewers who offered encouragement and suggestions for
enhancing this volume. Jonathan Fife, editor, and Bryan Hollister, managing editor, of the ASHE-ERIC Higher Education
Reports, were always ready with immediate assistance and
willing cooperation in my researching and writing this
volume.

INTRODUCTION

Reconciling the rights and responsibilities of colleges and universities with those of their students during recent years has been troublesome for numerous higher education administrators as they have sought to resolve conflicts between institutions and students. Students continue to bring legal actions against their colleges and universities, contending that administrative policies and practice often conflict directly with their personal constitutional rights. Conversely, administrators have documented that their responsibilities as institutional officials require them to consider the prerogatives of their colleges and universities in designing and implementing policy.

Students continue to bring legal actions against their colleges and universities, contending that administrative policies and practice often conflict directly with their personal constitutional rights.

Offensive Speech on Campus

The continuing and nationally publicized debates and controversies over the regulation of students' offensive speech at the University of Michigan, Brown University, Stanford University, and the University of Wisconsin system, among others, illustrate the seriousness of the conflicts involving First Amendment issues of speech and the corresponding need for colleges and universities to maintain an atmosphere appropriate and necessary for normal campus activities.

Some colleges and universities, in response to incidents on campus involving abuse directed by students to other students, have established policies for remedying such personally abusive and derogatory remarks. Other institutions are considering the merits of incorporating regulations against hate speech and are investigating whether they are the appropriate way to address the problem. To date, three prominent cases, all involving public institutions of higher education, have addressed directly the constitutionality of policies and administrative practices restricting speech: legal actions brought by students against the University of Michigan, the University of Wisconsin system, and George Mason University. Moreover, the U.S. Supreme Court has ruled that speech cannot be regulated on the basis of only certain categories.

This volume synthesizes the contemporary literature, including case law, and the resulting general principles that can be applied to future policies and practice when balancing the rights of students and the responsibilities of colleges and universities for ensuring an environment where all students can participate in the intellectual and physical boundaries of the campus.

Privately supported colleges and universities, although not generally under constitutional mandate, might find it desirable to appraise the merits of providing the same rights to their students as do state, or public, institutions. In addition to contractual considerations, privately supported colleges or universities still must deal with issues of institutional "self" respect, educational mission, and students' expectations, among others.

Students' Right of Association and Assembly

Closely related to the issue of what constitutes free speech and its limits is the parallel constitutional guarantee of freedom of assembly and association. Gay student groups, student religious groups, and Greek social groups continue to charge college and university administrators with denying their rights and privileges of recognition that other, less controversial, groups receive.

Still other students have found that on some campuses demonstrations are allowed against attempts to curtail academic programs but not against apartheid in South Africa, for example. On some campuses, demonstrations are allowed to protest decisions regarding tenure for the faculty but not demonstrations in favor of or against abortion. It is therefore realistic to conclude that a paramount problem among college officials is "how to balance the claims of freedom and responsibility on the campus" (Carnegie Foundation 1990, p. 1).

Testing College Athletes for Drugs

Another prominent clash between higher education's institutional responsibilities and students' individual rights is mandatory drug testing of college athletes. College and university administrators to date have failed to convince most courts that their mandatory drug tests constitute responsible administrative policy and practice, because their testing programs have invaded students' rights of privacy and fair treatment. Institutions, further, are finding themselves between their students and the National Collegiate Athletic Association (NCAA), as the national athletic umbrella organization also has failed to convince the courts that it has a compelling need to force students to be tested for drugs.

Reasons for such testing vary, but, generally, the NCAA contends that testing, in addition to protecting the health and safety of athletes, ensures fair and equitable competition. Colleges and universities have cited concerns about public policy as their primary reasons for drug testing when they have conducted their own programs, either separate from or in addition to the NCAA's testing requirements. Students object to these reasons on the basis that their being forced to undergo testing before being found responsible for a drug violation represents an invasion of their personal privacy and an unfair violation of trust. They find the mandatory testing degrading, humiliating, and offensively intrusive, and most of the nation's courts that have considered such claims have agreed.

Evidence indicates that some colleges and universities are beginning to reconcile students' rights with institutional responsibilities by employing an educational rationale, as well as legal considerations, when determining the merits of mandatory testing programs. For example, Stanford University took the posture of its student athletes against the NCAA's position, and the University of Washington dropped all mandatory components of its testing program and revised its policies to require testing only for athletes suspected of using drugs. It has established comprehensive drug education programs for all entering students as well as for student athletes. Students who object to testing, however, continue to charge other colleges and universities in the courts, and these legal claims are in various stages of litigation.

This volume traces the evolution to date of the courts' decisions regarding the issues of mandatory drug testing of college student athletes. These rulings can serve as principles, as well as legal precedent, for college and university administrators in their own understanding of the merit, or lack of merit, of drug testing on their own campuses.

Students' Safety and Security

Still another troublesome area for college and university administrators is the problem of increasing crime on campus and institutional liability for their students' safety on campus. A national study of college campuses found a 26 percent increase, over the preceding five years, in the number of crimes reported on campus, and 47 percent of college and university presidents said that crime was a "moderate" to "major" problem on their campuses (Carnegie Foundation 1990, p. 41).

Students who sue colleges and universities for the harm to them resulting from crime or injuries sustained on campus generally claim the harm resulted because of the institution's negligence. In what ways are courts holding colleges liable for the safety and security of their students? This question is approached in this report through an analysis of court rulings regarding liability for sexual attacks on campus, injuries to students not involving assaults, alcohol-related injuries, and institutional defenses against students' charges of negligence.

In liability cases involving crime on campus, the courts in numerous jurisdictions have acknowledged the dependent status of students in relation to their colleges. They have used concepts of landlord/tenant and business/invitee, among others, to describe the relationship between college and student. If the college-student relationship is "sufficiently special," it appears that courts are willing to hold institutions to a duty of care, particularly if the harm is reasonably foreseeable. The concept of foreseeability involves the extent to which an institution knew, or should have known, that a student was exposed, or could be exposed, to a risk of injury.

Students, to prove that the college or university was negligent, have had to show the courts that the institution owed them a duty of care, that a breach of the duty caused them actual harm, and that the institution's conduct or lack thereof was the proximate reason for the harm.

Reconciling Rights and Responsibilities
The focus of this volume, in considering the primary issues revolving around reconciling the rights and responsibilities of colleges and universities with the rights of students in these areas, is on two questions:

1. What do college and university administrators need to know?
2. What principles should they follow in establishing policies for administrative practice?

Reporting and synthesizing applicable case law provide a pragmatic way to learn about the problems and to acquire the background knowledge necessary to deal with them. Further, the cases depict the reality of contemporary college life. They provide a window for studying students' and institutions' prerogatives when they appear to collide with each other.

Can college and university administrators design policies to accommodate the rights of students and the educational

responsibilities of their institutions? The educational considerations and legal principles that have evolved from precedent
established in the cases adjudicated to date help to provide
the foundation for future policy and practice in our colleges
and universities.

OFFENSIVE SPEECH ON CAMPUS: Is Regulation the Answer?

The number of verbal and physical incidents directed toward minority students and student groups spiraled during the late 1980s, and African-American students in particular have been the recipients of targeted abuse. Forty-eight percent of the presidents of the nation's research and doctorate-granting universities acknowledged in one report that "racial intimidation/harassment was a 'moderate' to 'major' problem on their campuses" (Carnegie Foundation 1990, p. 18).

In response to incidents involving verbal abuse directed by students toward other students, many colleges and universities have created policies, or codes, as a remedy for abusive and derogatory remarks that offend students. Still other institutions are considering the merits of incorporating these anti–hate speech regulations and are investigating whether they are the appropriate way to address the problem.

One of the most important issues for college and university administrators considering speech policies is the question of constitutionality. The three institutional cases and their outcomes discussed in this section provide guiding principles in public colleges' and universities' determining the permissibility of speech regulations. These rulings constitute the cases involving higher education institutions litigated to date. The three examples—the University of Michigan, the Wisconsin system, and George Mason University—either promulgated regulations to restrict offensive speech or regulated speech in absence of a policy. Students contended that the institutional sanctions were unconstitutional invasions of their freedom of speech, and the respective courts' analyses are discussed in this section. The city of St. Paul case involving speech that offends on the basis of only certain categories also is discussed, as the Supreme Court's ruling will affect state colleges and universities.

The University of Michigan's Policy

The University of Michigan in 1987 became increasingly concerned about the rising tide of racial intolerance and harassment on campus. Incidents on campus had included unknown persons who distributed flyers declaring "open season" on African-Americans, a student disc jockey at an on-campus radio station who allowed racist jokes to be broadcast, and a Ku Klux Klan uniform that was displayed from a dormitory window (*Doe* v. *University of Michigan* 1989, p. 854).

In response to these and other racial incidents, a proposed policy by Michigan's acting president was distributed to various campus constituencies and published in the *University Record.* Faculty, students, and staff were invited to comment, and public hearings on the proposed policy were held before the policy's submission to the Regents. An interpretive guide with examples of sanctionable conduct also was planned to serve as an authoritative guide for the campus community.

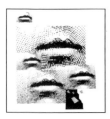

The policy became effective in 1988. It "prohibited any individual's behavior, verbal or physical, under the penalty of sanctions, if it stigmatizes or victimizes an individual on the basis of race, ethnicity, religion, sex, sexual orientation, creed, national origin, ancestry, age, marital status, handicap, or Vietnam-era veteran status" (*Doe* 1989, p. 856).

A psychology graduate student, Doe, maintained that some controversial theories positing biologically based differences between sexes and races might be perceived as "sexist" and "racist" by some students, and he feared that discussion of these theories might be sanctionable under the policy. He further asserted that his right to freely and openly discuss these theories was impermissibly restricted, and he requested that the policy be declared unconstitutional on the grounds of vagueness and overbreadth. The university responded that the policy was never intended to be applied to sanctioning classroom discussion of legitimate ideas. The federal district court disagreed, however, because in the guide, which suggested the kinds of examples that would be sanctionable, an explicitly stated example of sanctionable conduct was the following:

> *A male student makes remarks in class like "Women just aren't as good in this field as men," thus creating a hostile learning atmosphere for female classmates* (*Doe* 1989, p. 860).

A review of the university's complaint files on discriminatory harassment found that, on at least three occasions, students had been disciplined or threatened with discipline for comments made in a classroom. Further, another student was disciplined because he stated in the context of a social work research class that he believed that homosexuality was a disease that could be psychologically treated. The court con-

cluded that Doe's fears of prosecution were justified because
the policy had been enforced broadly and indiscriminately.

Speech versus conduct

In addressing the constitutionality of Michigan's policy, the
federal district court first distinguished between speech,
which is generally protected by the First Amendment, and
conduct. It emphasized that conduct is what the university
may legitimately regulate. For example, discrimination in
employment, education, and government benefits on the basis
of race, sex, ethnicity, and religion are prohibited by the Constitution as well as by both state and federal statutes (*Doe*
1989, p. 861). In addition, many forms of sexually abusive
and harassing conduct, such as rape and other forms of criminal sexual conduct, are also sanctionable.

A civil remedy under Title VII exists for women who are
subjected to demands for sexual favors by employers, and
minorities or women who are exposed to such extreme and
pervasive harassment in the workplace as to create a hostile
or offensive working environment are also entitled to civil
damages. The court was clear that the First Amendment presents no barrier to the establishment of internal university
sanctions as to any of these categories of conduct over and
above any remedies already provided by laws. When the issue
moves to speech, however, the public college or university
has limited power to regulate so-called "pure speech."

Overbreadth

With regard to the University of Michigan's policy, the graduate student claimed that it was invalid because it was overbroad. The court acknowledged that a fundamental principle
of American democracy is that statutes regulating First Amendment activities must be narrowly drawn to address "only the
specific evil at hand" (*Doe* 1989, p. 864).

> *A law regulating speech will be deemed overbroad if it
> sweeps within its ambit a substantial amount of protected
> speech along with that which it may legitimately regulate
> (Broadrick v. Oklahoma 1973, p. 612).*

The U.S. Supreme Court has ruled consistently that statutes
punishing speech or conduct solely on the grounds that they
are unseemly or offensive are unconstitutionally overbroad.

In other words, the state and, in this situation, its university may not prohibit broad classes of speech if in doing so a substantial amount of constitutionally protected conduct is also prohibited. This flaw was the policy's fundamental one, according to the court (*Doe* 1989, p. 864). It swept within its scope a significant amount of "verbal conduct" that was protected speech under the First Amendment and therefore was ruled overbroad. While the University of Michigan had a legitimate need—and right—to address the rising tide of racial intolerance and harassment on its campus, it did not have a right to establish an antidiscrimination policy that had the effect of prohibiting certain speech because it disagreed with ideas or messages sought to be conveyed, even when large numbers of people found that speech offensive, even gravely so.

Vagueness
In addition to the claim of overbreadth, John Doe also contended that Michigan's policy was impermissibly vague. It is generally accepted that a statute is unconstitutionally vague when "men of common intelligence must necessarily guess at its meaning" (*Broadrick* 1973, p. 607). Further, a statute must give adequate warning of the conduct that is to be prohibited and must state clearly the standards for those who are to apply them.

When the court examined the policy, "it was simply impossible to discern any limitation on its scope or any conceptual distinction between protected and unprotected conduct" (*Doe* 1989, p. 867). For example, one section of the policy required that language must "stigmatize" or "victimize" an individual to be sanctionable. Both of these terms, however, are general and elude precise definition. What one individual might find victimizing or stigmatizing, another individual might not. According to the court:

> *It is clear that the fact that a statement may victimize or stigmatize an individual does not, in and of itself, strip it of protection under the accepted First Amendment tests* (*Doe* 1989, p. 867).

Still another element of the policy troubling to the court was its pronouncement that for conduct to be sanctionable, the stigmatizing and victimizing statements had to "involve an express or implied threat to an individual's academic efforts, employment, participation in University-sponsored extracurricular activities, or personal safety." The court was unable to discern what kind of conduct would constitute a "threat" to an individual's academic efforts. The policy was not clear in concept or intent.

The *Doe* court concluded that the university failed to articulate any meaningful way to distinguish sanctionable from protected speech. University students of common understanding were forced to guess at whether a comment or statement about a controversial issue would later be found to be sanctionable under the policy. The court thus ruled that the terms of the policy were so vague that its enforcement would be unconstitutional. While it proclaimed empathy with the University of Michigan's obligation to ensure equal educational opportunities for all its students, the court nonetheless stressed with equal empathy that such efforts could not be at the expense of free speech.

The University of Wisconsin Rule

Following a series of incidents of racial harassment on the University of Wisconsin at Madison campus, the university's Board of Regents adopted a policy in 1989, known as the UW Rule, that regulated discriminatory and harassing behavior on its campuses. Conscious of the University of Michigan case, the University of Wisconsin system adopted what it considered a more narrowly drawn rule that focused on harassing speech directed at individuals with an intent to do them some type of harm. The governing board excluded restrictions on classroom discussions and limits on displays or distribution of literature (Hodulik 1990).

The UW Rule, in brief, provided that the university could discipline a student in nonacademic matters for comments, epithets, or other expressive behavior if it:

1. *was racist or discriminatory;*
2. *was directed at an individual;*
3. *demeaned the race, sex, religion, color, creed, disability, sexual orientation, national origin, ancestry, or age of the individual addressed; and*
4. *created an intimidating, hostile, or demeaning environment for education, university-related work, or other university-authorized activity (UWM Post v. Board of Regents of University of Wisconsin 1991, p. 1166)*

Just like the University of Michigan earlier, the University of Wisconsin system also circulated to the campus communities a brochure explaining the rule and providing guidance as to its scope and application.

In early 1990, the *UWM Post* and others (plaintiffs) brought suit against the University of Wisconsin Board of Regents, claiming that the UW Rule violated their right of free speech guaranteed by the First Amendment as well as their right to due process and equal protection guaranteed by the Fourteenth Amendment. They argued that the UW Rule was overbroad because it was a content-based rule regulating a substantial amount of protected speech and also that it was vague because terms used in the policy ("discriminatory comments, epithets, or other expressive behavior" and "demean") were unduly vague. Finally, the plaintiffs contended that the UW Rule did not make clear whether the prohibited speech must actually create a hostile educational environment or whether a speaker must merely intend to create such an environment.

The federal district court acknowledged the great importance of protecting speech from content-based regulations and used an earlier Supreme Court ruling as rationale for its own conclusions in that particular situation.

Above all else, the First Amendment means that government has no power to restrict expression because of its message, its ideas, its subject matter, or its content. To permit the continued building of our politics and culture, and to assure self-fulfillment for each individual, our people are guaranteed the right to express any thought, free from government censorship. The essence of this forbidden censorship is content control. Any restriction on expressive activity because of its content would completely undercut the "profound national commitment to the principle that debate on public issues would be uninhibited, robust, and wide open" (Police Department of Chicago v. Mosley 1972, p. 95).

In the situation involving the UW Rule, the Wisconsin Board of Regents maintained that its policy was within the scope of "fighting words" and thus not protected by the First Amendment. The federal district court, however, found that, because "the elements of the UW Rule do not require that the regulated speech, by its very utterance, tend to incite violent reaction, the rule goes beyond the present scope of the fighting words doctrine" (*UWM Post* 1991, p. 1172). The court supported its rationale by addressing each of the four elements of the UW Rule:

The first element of the UW Rule, which requires that the speech be racist or discriminatory, describes the content of the speech to be regulated but does not state that the speech must tend to cause a breach of the peace.

The second element, which requires that the speech be directed at an individual, meets the requirement . . . that the speech be "directed to the person of the hearer." In addition, the second element makes it likely that the rule will cover some speech [that] tends to incite violent reaction. Nevertheless, this element does not require that the regulated speech always *tend to incite such reaction and is likely to allow the rule to apply to many situations where a breach of the peace is unlikely to occur.*

The third element of the UW Rule requires that the regulated speech demean an individual's race, sex, religion, etc. . . . Nonetheless, the third element . . . does not address the concerns of . . . [all] the fighting words definition (words [that] by their very utterance tend to incite an immediate breach of the peace). Speech may demean an individual's characteristics without tending to incite that individual or others to an immediate breach of the peace.

The fourth element of the UW Rule requires that the prohibited speech create an intimidating, hostile, or demeaning environment. [Such an environment] certainly "disturbs the public peace or tranquility . . . of a [university] community." However, it does not necessarily tend to incite violent reaction. . . . [T]he term "hostile" covers nonviolent as well as violent situations. . . . This court cannot properly find that an intimidating or demeaning environment tends to incite an immediate breach of the peace (UWM Post 1991, pp. 1172–73).

When considering the four elements of the policy in total, the court concluded that the UW Rule impermissibly regulated speech based on its content. It is best illustrated, according to the court, by the fact that the rule disciplines students whose comments, epithets, or other expressive behavior demeans their addressees' race, sex, religion, and so on, but it leaves unregulated those comments, epithets, and other expressive behaviors that affirm or do not address an individual's race, sex, religion, and so on. The UW Rule is therefore "overbroad and thus in violation of the First Amendment" (*UWM Post* 1991, p. 1177).

George Mason University's Approach to Regulation
Unlike the University of Michigan's and University of Wisconsin's policies directed toward curbing offensive speech, the legal challenge against George Mason University was for its discipline of students who dressed as "ugly women." The students in Iota Xi Chapter of Sigma Chi Fraternity charged that the university unconstitutionally punished their expression protected by the First Amendment.

The incident in question involved fraternity members who, during their chapter's annual celebration of Derby Days, held a "Dress a Sig" competition in which they dressed as caricatures of "ugly women." The students had earlier sought the usual university approval for this celebration, and the proposed program had undergone several changes. No university-required changes were applied to the "ugly woman" contest, however, and the event took place in the cafeteria of the student union building.

In the "Dress a Sig" competition, a participant dressed in black face, used pillows to represent breasts and buttocks, and wore a black wig and curlers. A week later, several George Mason student leaders wrote the dean of students requesting the imposition of sanctions on the fraternity, "as the 'Dress a Sig' contest had offended them because it perpetuated racial and sexual stereotypes" (*Iota Xi Chapter of Sigma Chi Fraternity* v. *George Mason University* 1991, p. 793). Almost immediately, the dean of students announced, then clarified in a letter, that the fraternity and its members would be disciplined by being placed on probation for two years. During this probationary period, the fraternity would not be allowed to hold social or sports activities.

When considering the disciplinary action of George Mason and the students' contention that the university's response was unconstitutional, the federal district court emphasized that, although a state university may place appropriate restrictions on free expression as to time, place, and manner, George Mason University did not seek to regulate any conduct whatsoever.

*It was not the conduct of renting the auditorium, holding
Derby Days, raising money for charity, providing entertain-
ment, or performing a skit [that] prompted GMU to discipline the members of Sigma Chi. To the contrary, it was the
expressive message conveyed by the skit [that] was perceived
as offensive by several student groups [that] prompted GMU
to discipline the fraternity (Iota Xi Chapter 1991, p. 794).*

In this particular situation, George Mason had disciplined
fraternity members because their activity was considered
offensive, not because the members violated any regulations
on time, place, or manner established by the university for
the contest's activity. Quoting the Supreme Court in *Texas
v. Johnson* (1989), the district court reaffirmed that "[i]f there
is a bedrock principle underlying the First Amendment, it is
that the Government may not prohibit the expression of an
idea simply because society finds the idea itself offensive or
disagreeable" (p. 795). The U.S. Supreme Court has not
veered from this principle and, in fact, has not recognized
an exception, even when the American flag was burned in
the *Texas* case.

In conclusion, George Mason University may not discipline
students by infringing on their First Amendment rights based
on the perceived offensive content of an activity. Although
the university disagreed with the message conveyed by the
fraternity's activity, the "First Amendment does not recognize
exceptions for bigotry, racism, and religious intolerance or
ideas or matters some [might] deem trivial, vulgar, or pro-
fane" (*Iota Xi Chapter* 1991, p. 795).

George Mason University, in early 1992, registered an
appeal of the district court's ruling, but to date the appellate
court has taken no action.

*". . . [i]f there
is a bedrock
principle
underlying
the First
Amendment,
it is that the
Government
may not
prohibit the
expression of
an idea simply
because
society finds
the idea itself
offensive or
disagreeable."*

Supreme Court Signals Reexamination
Of Speech Codes

The U.S. Supreme Court ruled on June 22, 1992, that cities
and states, and thus state colleges and universities, may not
prohibit speech on the basis of the subjects the speech
addresses (*R.A.V. v. St. Paul, Minn.* 1992). The ruling evolved
from charges brought two years earlier by the city of St. Paul
against a teenager who burned a cross in the yard of an
African-American family that had moved into an all-white
neighborhood. The 17-year-old was cited with violating the

city's law prohibiting the display of anything that "arouses anger, alarm, or resentment in others on the basis of race, color, creed, religion, or gender" (*R.A.V.* 1992, p. 4667). The law specifically named cross burnings and displays of the Nazi swastika as examples of such prohibition.

The Minnesota Supreme Court upheld the St. Paul law, finding that it applied only to expressions that constituted "fighting words," a category of expression not protected by the First Amendment. The nation's highest court disagreed, however, and ruled that the term "fighting words" does not allow the government to punish the use of some words and not others. In this situation, for example, St. Paul contended that because "fighting words" are not constitutionally protected, it could punish people who used particular "fighting words" that the city considered specifically harmful to certain groups. The city law in this instance punished expression that caused anger or alarm or resentment on the basis of race, color, religion, or gender. In declaring the city law unconstitutional, the U.S. Supreme Court said:

> *[Under the law,] those who wish to use "fighting words" in connection with other ideas—to express hostility, for example, on the basis of political affiliation, union membership, or homosexuality—are not covered. The First Amendment does not permit St. Paul to impose special prohibitions on those speakers who express views on disfavored subjects* (*R.A.V.* 1992, p. 4671).

Justice Antonin Scalia, writing for the majority of the Supreme Court, stated, "Selectivity of this sort creates the possibility that the government is seeking to handicap the expression of particular ideas" (p. 4672). Such proscription, ruled the Supreme Court, is invalid.

This latest ruling appears to place the focus of institutional policies on actions—not speech—such as physical disruption or assault, regardless of the motive involved. Indeed, the Supreme Court acknowledged that the city of St. Paul had sufficient means at its disposal to prevent undesirable behavior like cross burning, including laws against damage to property, arson, and terrorism. The logical application of this ruling to policies at state colleges and universities is that punishment should be "without reference to the content of the words, or the thought—hateful or benign—that [might] have impelled the disrupter" (O'Neil 1992, p. A40). Robert M. O'Neil, legal scholar, former university president, and founding director of the Thomas Jefferson Center for the Protection of Free Expression, summarized the task for institutional administrators when he reflected that colleges and universities do not need the Supreme Court to teach them to focus on offensive actions rather than words.

We should have been teaching that lesson all along both on our campuses and to the rest of the world, where the reluctance to suppress ideas—particularly hateful ideas—is less readily apparent. But the Court may have helped us to take stock of our own goals and what methods we need to achieve them (O'Neil 1992, p. A40).

Status of Attempts at Regulation
These three institutions' experiences and the recent Supreme Court ruling that declared unconstitutional St. Paul's law that punished for displays of bias, including cross burning, provide considerable insight as to how future courts will view anti-speech policies. Some guiding principles are available for public college and university officials who are considering policies:

- Speech or expression may not be punished on the basis of the subjects the speech addresses. The government must be neutral when it regulates speech.
- Overbroad policies regulating speech are prohibited.
- Unduly vague policies regulating speech are prohibited.
- Restrictions as to time, place, and manner on speech or expression appropriate for the educational environment and for maintaining order on the campus are constitutional.
- Policies based on "fighting words," even in part, cannot discriminate on the basis of content or viewpoint.
- Due process protections and procedures should be in place before and followed during any disciplinary process.

Even though privately supported colleges and universities generally are not held to constitutional requirements in dealing with their students, they still must address issues of institutional image, "self" respect, and students' expectations. Is the private college's mission any less than the public college's purpose? Is the relationship between institution and student different? Many private colleges and universities might decide their interests will be served best by providing the same rights to their students as do public institutions.

Is Regulation the Path to Civility?

The contemporary literature, the available cases, and interviews with college and university administrators reveal that many of the issues surrounding policies restricting speech relate to philosophical and pragmatic concerns as well as to constitutional questions.

Even if colleges and universities should be able to narrowly tailor policies to regulate expression, such policies most likely will fail to reach some of the most prominent forms of racial, gender-based, and other epithets and harassment, such as those broadcast on posters and flyers and during social activities and events (Brownstein 1991a; Byrne 1991; Siegel 1990). Whatever the heightened level of technical and educational expertise administrators might acquire in designing policies regulating speech, hate speech may be prohibited in certain circumstances but not others. And perhaps most important, "where to begin" and "where to end" with proscriptive policies are fundamental issues. Are higher education institutions concerned only with racial, religious, or gender-based slurs? Many college and university students are also gravely offended when an epithet is directed toward their mother or if they are called "fat" or "stupid." It is difficult to discern the specific terms that would be demeaning within a particular student body.

Another troublesome concern relates to the position that policies restricting speech, even if constitutional, do not deal with "root" causes of racism, sexism, or other forms of harassment (Baruch 1990; Gunther 1990; O'Neil 1991b; Strossen 1990). Numerous scholars and commentators have argued that education—not regulations, codes, and discipline—is the route to destroying prejudice and bigotry. In fact, disciplinary rules might be the least effective way an educational institution can promote tolerance among its members. Rules prohibiting offensive remarks, slurs, or epithets often cause racism and racial harassment to go underground or surface in other, different forms. This view mandates that educational institutions employ definitive and forceful programs and activities to educate students—indeed, the entire campus community—about tolerance for people who hold various racial, cultural, ethnic, and religious heritages.

If the first concern relates to lack of comprehensiveness and the second to lack of a relationship between treatment and cure, a third disturbing aspect of speech policies focuses on what some educators have labeled "shortsightedness"— the contention that colleges and universities cannot and should not attempt to force their students to accept those ideas or conform to the ideas that they consider appropriate for maintaining order and educational decorum on their campuses (Carnegie Foundation 1990; Gale 1991; Weinberg 1991).

A prohibition of speech, even offensive or hate speech, by whatever definition, places colleges and universities in the position of censors and proclaimers of which speech is deemed worthy and which is not. The Carnegie Foundation's special report on campus life concluded from its national study that policies on speech might be expedient, even sincere and well meaning, but they do not provide a satisfactory response to offensive language. What higher education institutions "can and should do is define high standards of civility and condemn, in the strongest possible terms, any violation of such standards" (1990, p. 20).

Compelling Reasons for Speech Policies

As the courts to date have ruled overwhelmingly that speech policies at state colleges and universities are unconstitutional, what are the most significant, perhaps compelling, reasons *for* such policies that educators and others continue to espouse? One of the two primary arguments is that students who are the targets of insults, catcalls, or other assaultive speech, particularly minority students, suffer pain and injury as the result of that speech (Delgado 1991; Lawrence 1990; Matsuda 1989; Post 1991). Abusive words are humiliating and can have long-term damaging effects on the victim (Greenawalt 1990).

Hate speech erodes the victim's sense of self, creates fear, and restricts movement. Most of all, it inflicts pain, silences the individual, and undermines one's confidence and security (Matsuda 1989). And when victims of abusive speech are silenced, they have no realistic forum or opportunity for counterexpression. Offensive or hate speech does not attempt to connect the speaker and the addressee; thus, it does nothing to encourage the discussion of ideas between them. "More speech" is rarely a solution. Epithets typically strike suddenly, immobilizing their victims and rendering them speechless. In most situations, "members of minority groups realize that they are likely to lose if they fight back, and they are forced to remain silent and submissive" (Lawrence 1990, p. 13).

In addition to the pain and injury of students who are targets of abusive speech, numerous college and university administrators further maintain that such speech causes harm to the educational environment and to the institution's mission. It is, in fact, the prevention of this harm that is central to many, if not most, speech regulations specific to a campus (Hodulik 1990; Napier 1991; Shapiro 1990). Racist expression in particular interferes with education, not only because of harm that it inflicts on individuals or groups or the marketplace of ideas, but also because it "exemplifies conduct that is contrary to the educational values that colleges or universities seek to instill" (Laney 1990). This argument for speech policies, however compelling, focuses on colleges' goals and prerogatives to foster an educational environment that is comfortable to *all* who have earned the right to be part of that community—women, African-Americans, and other minorities. And campus policies, even policies restricting speech, often are necessary for the institution to maintain an educational environment conducive to learning and for it to fulfill its mission.

Educational Approaches
The growing body of literature relating to offensive speech on college campuses emphasizes the merits of educational approaches rather than disciplinary means to address problems of racial harassment. Orientation programs for entering students, ongoing seminars and forums on racism for all students, and multicultural education workshops for faculty, staff, and administrators would be appropriate beginning institutional responses.

Numerous educators have called for required courses in the history of racism and the civil rights movement in the United States, cultural diversity, gender, race, and religious prejudice, and the psychology and sociology of attitude and value development, among other topics. Beginning with academic year 1992–93, every freshman student who enters the University of California–Berkeley must take a course focusing on how American history, society, and identity have been shaped by the nation's diverse cultural population (*Chronicle of Higher Education* 1992c).

While such required courses are controversial among some institutions and their faculty members, a trend is developing toward incorporating requirements for racial and ethnic studies, similar to Berkeley's requirement for "American Cultures," in the undergraduate curriculum at many colleges and universities.

The primary goals are not so much to punish, but to deter, offensive or hate speech and to deal, from the perspective of educational development, with the attitudes and intolerance that trigger such slurs and comments (Baruch 1990; Byrne 1991; Strossen 1990). Students' use of epithets or similar speech in the classroom, for example, might best be dealt with by faculty. A faculty member's authority in the classroom does not depend on sanctions, and a faculty member's responsibility for addressing offensive speech enhances the prospect that the problem will be recognized and approached as an educational one (American Association of University 1992; Ehrlich and Scimecca 1991; Smolla 1990).

Outside the classroom, where campus regulations regarding behavior still apply, an advantage of educational approaches is that they can avoid creating disciplinary boundaries for forbidden or prohibited speech. The focus would be on understanding the reasons for prejudice and bigotry and the development of sensitivity to and tolerance for other people and other cultures. Student organizations, as part of their annual recognition or registration process, could be responsible for conducting educational activities and programs for their members that focus on cultural diversity. The college or university union might sponsor campuswide educational activities, and residence life programs likewise might include appropriate learning experiences for the residents directed toward curtailing racism and sexism.

Perhaps one of the most effective approaches an institution can take regarding hate speech is that its leaders speak out frequently and forcefully to denounce abusive speech. College and university presidents, in particular, can issue definitive statements, as well as symbolic ones, by strongly and publicly denouncing speech that is intended to insult, intimidate, or harm another human being. Student leaders and respected student members of majority groups on campus can be effective in speaking out against abusive speech, and they often can be successful in peer education activities for student organizations and other students.

Summary

Because offensive speech is defined by its content, state college and university regulations to prohibit it raise important questions with regard to boundaries and interpretations of the First Amendment. To date, three federal district courts have ruled against higher education institutions' prohibiting offensive, or hate, speech. One court went even farther, declaring that the Wisconsin Rule that regulated offensive speech did as much to hurt diversity on campus as it did to help it.

> *By establishing content-based restrictions on speech, the rule limits the diversity of ideas among students and thereby prevents the "robust exchange of ideas" [that] intellectually diverse campuses provide* (*UWM Post* 1991, p. 1176).

In addition to these unsuccessful attempts to regulate speech by two state universities and one statewide university system, the U.S. Supreme Court likewise has ruled invalid the government's (St. Paul's) attempt to regulate expression when the prohibition is on the basis of race, color, religion, or gender. It thus seems unlikely that state colleges and universities in the future can constitutionally regulate speech, because, at least to date, such regulations have punished expression that offends on the basis of only certain categories—race and gender, for example.

Content-neutral expression, however, can be regulated as to its location, time, and manner when the expression is incompatible with the lawful functions within the state college's or university's mission and scope. Any expression that materially disrupts class work, poses a clear and present danger of violence, or involves substantial disorder or invasion of the rights of others is not protected under the First Amendment.

It is significant that higher education institutions have not explored fully the parameters of codes and nonspeech sanctions surrounding *behavior*. It could be time to deemphasize speech and emphasize education, tolerance, civility, and responsible behavior.

STUDENT GROUPS: Rights of Association and Assembly

While the freedom of association is not explicitly set out in the First Amendment, it has long been held to be implicit in the freedoms of speech, assembly, and petition. The U.S. Supreme Court again affirmed this constitutional right—this time for college and university students—when it ruled that Central Connecticut State College could not deny recognition to a local chapter of Students for a Democratic Society (*Healy* v. *James* 1972).

In *Healy,* the students who attempted to organize a local SDS group followed the established college procedures and filed a request with the Student Affairs Committee for official recognition as a campus organization. The committee, with some reservations initially, ultimately approved the application and recommended to the president of the college that the group be given official recognition. The president determined that the group's philosophy was at odds with the college's commitment to academic freedom and that the organization would be a disruptive influence on the campus. The Supreme Court rejected the president's position and ruled that "the denial of official recognition, without justification, to college organizations burdens or abridges that associational right" (*Healy* 1972, p. 2339). While affirming the institution's right to require that student groups agree to adhere to institutional regulations, the *Healy* ruling is likewise clear that state colleges or universities may not deny recognition to student groups simply because they find the views expressed by them abhorrent.

Benefits of Recognition

Courts have interpreted the official recognition of groups to mean that the college or university acknowledges and sanctions the existence of the group, not that it necessarily approves any of the organization's religious, political, economic, or philosophical positions. Some colleges and universities during the past decade began to use the term "registering" in place of "recognizing" student organizations, but such labels or terms do not alter the meaning of *what* such recognition means. Official recognition usually conveys various tangible benefits and privileges available at the institution only to recognized, or registered, groups. Such benefits might include:

1. The privilege of scheduling campus facilities for meetings and activities, usually rent free;
2. The option of leasing a campus post office box;
3. The right to request funds from the student activities fee;
4. Access to secretarial services;
5. The opportunity to use school media;
6. The right to post notices and to advertise on campus;
7. The privilege of being listed in the student handbook and yearbook;
8. The opportunity to qualify for awards and honors available to college student organizations; and
9. The option to use available office space (Gibbs 1989a, p. 35).

Although a college's or university's endorsement of a recognized student group is intangible—an expression of official neutrality—the benefits associated with that recognition are tangible and often necessary for the organization to function just like any other student organization on campus.

Gay/Lesbian Student Groups

Among the most vocal students seeking recognition on college campuses during recent years have been the gay rights groups. They have desired the same status as other student groups to likewise receive the same tangible benefits. On campuses where institutional administrators have refused to recognize these gay student groups, they have based their denials on one or more of the following arguments:

1. Recognition would constitute endorsement of or give credibility to homosexual behavior.
2. Recognition would not be consistent with the educational mission of the college or university.
3. Recognition might create personal stress and anxiety for students who are troubled about their sexual identity.
4. Homosexuality is illegal.
5. The institution has a duty to promote the prevailing community values and standards.
6. Nonrecognition is not an infringement of constitutional rights.

The courts have been consistent in rejecting these reasons for denying recognition to student organizations. In fact, most courts have relied on the Supreme Court's ruling in *Tinker* v. *Des Moines Independent Community School District,* that:

> . . . [F]or a state college or university to justify prohibition of a particular expression of opinion, it must be able to show that its action was caused by something more than a mere desire to avoid the discomfort and unpleasantness that always accompany an unpopular viewpoint. Certainly where there is no finding and no showing that engaging in the forbidden conduct would "materially and substantially interfere with the requirements of appropriate discipline in the operation of the school," the prohibition cannot be sustained (*Tinker* 1969, p. 509).

The Oklahoma Supreme Court was even more definitive when it determined that the state's Board of Regents had not presented justifiable proof to back its position in its nonrecognition of a gay student organization.

> No abridgement of associational rights can be tolerated if the only competing interest is the university's opposition to the content of that expression.
>
> Where the denial of recognition is based on mere suspicion, unpopularity, and the fear of what might occur and is achieved by state action [that] burdens associational rights resulting in the lessening of an organization's ability to effectuate legal purposes, guaranteed freedoms have been violated (*Gay Activists Alliance* v. *Board of Regents of University of Oklahoma* 1981, p. 1122).

Although courts have been emphatic that institutional recognition does not imply support, agreement, or approval of the organization's purpose, they have been equally decisive that associational activities need not be tolerated "where they infringe reasonable campus rules, interrupt classes, or substantially interfere with the opportunities of other students to obtain an education" (*Healy* 1972, p. 2340). Colleges and universities are not required to recognize organizations, but once they choose to sanction some groups, legal precedent indicates that courts generally will mandate the recognition of all student groups, providing three criteria have been met. First, the group must have complied with all institutional requirements for procedures and processes relating to reg-

No abridgement of associational rights can be tolerated if the only competing interest is the university's opposition to the content of that expression.

ulation of time, place, and manner. Second, the group must not behave in such a way or demonstrate a danger of violence or disruption to the institution's educational purpose, and, third, neither the organization nor its members may violate the criminal law during or through a group function.

Equal Treatment

A 10-year-long gay rights legal battle involved two student groups that brought suit against Georgetown University, a private Jesuit institution, for its failure to recognize them and provide the benefits enjoyed by other student groups. To receive these benefits, including the use of campus facilities, both the student government and college policies required that student organizations be recognized. Georgetown refused to recognize the groups because their purposes and activities violated Catholic moral teaching (*Gay Rights Coalition of Georgetown University Law Center* v. *Georgetown University* 1987).

The student groups contended that, through this denial, Georgetown violated the District of Columbia's Human Rights Act, which prevents discrimination in educational institutions in the use of or access to facilities and services based on, among other things, sexual orientation (D.C. Code section 1-2520 [1987]). Both sides claimed victory when the District of Columbia Court of Appeals ruled that Georgetown must provide the groups the tangible services and facilities but did not require the bestowal of official recognition (*Gay Rights Coalition* 1987).

The importance of the Georgetown ruling is that when some student organizations are allowed access to facilities and services on their campuses, even when the institution is not an agency of the state, institutional administrators may consider it prudent to adhere to principles of equal treatment to all student organizations for such access, even though the group's basic purposes might not be considered within the religious tenets of the private institution. Whether or not human rights acts are involved, administrators should weigh the ethical and educational implications of their consistency in policy and in practice.

The Georgetown case pitted the public's interest in prohibiting discrimination on the basis of sexual orientation, on the one hand, against the Jesuit university's freedom of religious exercise, on the other (Dutile 1988). Georgetown did not have to use the official recognition label relative to the gay rights groups but did have to provide equal facilities, services, and benefits made available to all other groups. In addition, the institution had to pay the suing student groups' legal costs of approximately $500,000 as well as the costs of retaining its own team of defense lawyers (*Chronicle of Higher Education* 1988, p. 1).

Religious Groups

Colleges do not have to provide these privileges to student organizations, but once privileges are granted to one group on campus, they should be granted to all groups. Religious groups are no exception. In terms of freedom of speech, association, and assembly, religious speech on a state college campus should be treated no differently from secular speech.

The Supreme Court addressed this issue in *Widmar* v. *Vincent* (1981), when a recognized student religious group, Cornerstone, at the University of Missouri at Kansas City was denied continued access to campus facilities. The university had actively encouraged student organizations, had officially recognized more than 100 such groups, and had provided campus facilities for recognized groups on a regular basis. Each year Cornerstone applied for university space in which to conduct its meetings and had received permission to use the facilities for four continuous years. At the end of the fourth year, however, the university decided to enforce a Board of Trustees ruling of several years earlier that prohibited the use of the institution's buildings and grounds "for purposes of religious worship or religious teaching" (*Widmar* 1981, p. 272). The students filed suit against the university, alleging that the enforcement of the regulation, now restricting their access to campus facilities, was a violation of their constitutional rights to free speech and free exercise of religion. The university argued that the regulation and its enforcement were necessary to prevent state support of religion. The federal district court upheld the university, but the appellate court reversed the lower court, determining that the university's policy was unconstitutional, designed to regulate the content of speech without showing a justifiable compelling reason (*Chess* v. *Widmar* 1980). The court concluded, generally, that religious speech, like other speech, is guaranteed protection by the First Amendment. Likewise, freedom of association is no less protected when it advances religious beliefs than when it advances other beliefs.

When the case reached the Supreme Court, the nation's highest court agreed with the court of appeals:

> *Having created a forum generally open to student groups, a state university may not practice content-based exclusion of religious speech when that exclusion is not narrowly drawn to achieve a state interest in the separation of church and state (Widmar v. Vincent 1981, p. 264).*

Greek Organizations

Greek organizations have witnessed continuous growth in recent years, and this increase in membership has shown a corresponding increase in problems like alcohol abuse, hazing, and incidents of racism and sexism, among others.

Because individual fraternity and sorority chapters are not typical student organizations in that they also are part of a larger, national organization, their host institutions often do not recognize them in the same manner as other student organizations.

By 1989, 53 percent of reporting colleges and universities had adopted written documents describing the relationship between the institution and its Greek organizations and listing policies and regulations (Harvey 1990, p. 31). Institutions give various reasons for the need for such statements of the relationship:

1. Fraternities and sororities are social in nature and do not necessarily relate directly to the institution's educational mission.
2. Greek groups might have a right to exist on campus, but their policies of governance need to be definitive and clear, as their national organizations also have a legitimate interest in the chapter's governance.
3. The host institution needs to avoid legal liability for students' acts.
4. Fraternities and sororities might have houses on college property, or the houses might be owned by the institution, but such ownership raises potential issues involving landlord/tenant or business/invitee relationships (discussed in the section titled "Colleges' Exposure to Liability").

While some institutions have responded to these or similar concerns by abolishing their Greek organizations, most colleges and universities have taken steps to determine the nature of the relationship between themselves and their fraternities and sororities. For example, some colleges own individual fraternity and sorority houses. Others might not own individual houses but provide coordination or supervision over the Greek system through intrafraternity and Panhellenic councils or some other appropriate internal structure of governance. Some campuses allow individual chapter rooms in residence halls or in student union buildings. Regardless of the relationship, however, it must be communicated and understood by all those involved—students, administrators, faculty, alumni, and the national leadership of the chapters on campus.

Because alcohol and substance abuse is perhaps the most serious concern about Greek life, special care should be taken to create the process and procedures for addressing these and other concerns about conduct or discipline. Hazing, for example, is a major concern on numerous campuses. It is against the law in at least 30 states (Harvey 1990; Maloney 1988), and several other states are considering the adoption of such bans. Alcohol and drug laws, like prohibitions on hazing, differ from state to state, and colleges and universities should evaluate on an ongoing basis the impact of their state's laws on their educational and legal relationships with Greek organizations.

The problem of alcohol and substance abuse is not limited to Greek organizations. It is a major concern on college campuses in general and applicable to *all* student organizations. Alcohol and drug education programs thus should be targeted to all students and student organizations.

Likewise, when institutions of higher education address any societal issue, such as racism, sexual harassment, or hate speech, student Greek groups should be provided the same opportunities for learning while also being held to the same expectations and standards as other student organizations. The fact that they are primarily social in nature and somewhat private because of their affiliation with a national corporation does not negate institutional responsibility to provide the structure for promoting desirable learning and behavior among students. Such expectations can be included in, and indeed might constitute the rationale for formal establishment of, the institution's relationship with its Greek groups.

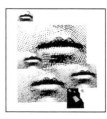

The CAS *Standards and Guidelines* (Council for the Advancement of Standards 1986) provide a contemporary framework for creating relationships between individual Greek organizations and an institution. Each institution might consider it helpful to have an umbrella document outlining the general relationship between it and its Greek student groups, as a system, and another document that individual chapters could amend or modify to accommodate their specific programs.

A review of 20 such college and university statements involving their fraternities and sororities reveals several similar inclusions: purpose of the institution; purposes of Greek organizations, including how they relate to the institution's purpose; a structure for accomplishing the local organization's purpose; conditions for institutional recognition or affiliation; the institution's responsibilities and obligations; the Greek organization's responsibilities and obligations; and a vehicle for modifying or altering an institution's relationships with its Greek organizations.

Student Assembly and Demonstrations

College administrators have discovered during recent years that students' rights of association and assembly are not confined to institutionally recognized student organizations. Students will assemble in large numbers on an ad hoc basis, often issue by issue, and campus demonstrations still take place. Much of the past decade, in fact, witnessed massive student demonstrations devoted to apartheid in South Africa and college and university policies and practices that sanctioned their investing in U.S. companies conducting business in South Africa. Some evidence suggests that these past demonstrations could be the prelude to future demonstrations focusing on abortion rights and the rights of a growing population exposed to and suffering from AIDS and/or HIV. Still other societal problems of racism, hate speech, and gender-related issues, to name a few, already are creating considerable activity on college and university campuses as students become involved in various philosophical and political positions. These points of debate often lead to unpredictable behavior from students, sometimes violent demonstrations, and frequent physical disturbances and destruction on campus.

Symbolic speech

Student demonstrations on campus, like other actions protected by the First Amendment, cannot be prohibited on the
basis of content or the message to be communicated. The
following paragraphs illustrate students' positions versus institutions' positions regarding demonstrations and related disputes and what the courts have said about the boundaries
of lawful campus demonstrations.

A student group at the University of Virginia protested the
political and racial environment in South Africa and the university's economic investment in that country by building
shanty-like structures on the front lawn of the University
Rotunda, where the Board of Visitors holds its meetings
(*Students Against Apartheid Coalition* v. *O'Neil* 1987a). They
asserted that the shanties were a form of symbolic speech that
is protected by the First Amendment. The university argued,
however, that the shanties were ugly and impaired the physical attractiveness of the campus. School administrators also
contended that it was lawful for them to restrict the time,
place, and manner of the students' expressive behavior to
maintain the architectural integrity and physical beauty of
the campus.

The federal district court ruled that:

> *Shanties constructed on the university lawn that were sym-
> bolic and life-size representations for illustrative, educative,
> and persuasive purposes of dwellings of black South Africa
> in ghettos of apartheid were forms of expressive symbolic
> communication that was protected by the First Amendment
> (*Students Against Apartheid Coalition* 1987a, p. 333).*

With regard to the university's restricting the erection of
the shanties on the lawn, however, the court stipulated that
the validity of the regulation regarding use of the lawn
depended on whether it was content neutral, was narrowly
tailored to meet a significant government interest, and left
open other channels of communication. In this situation, the
university's regulations were ruled to be impermissibly vague
as well as not constitutional, because they did not provide
students an ample alternative means to communicate their
message or opposition to apartheid. University of Virginia officials thus were forced to revise the regulations covering use
of the lawn. The federal district court ruled, four months fol-

lowing its first decision in favor of the students, that the university's revised policy regarding use of the lawn did not violate students' constitutional freedoms.

> *The University's revised lawn-use policy, which prohibited "structures," those physical objects [that] would interrupt architectural lines of historic area, from south side of Rotunda, did not violate First Amendment; policy was content neutral, precisely aimed at protecting university's aesthetic concern in architecture, and permitted students wide array of additional modes of communications (Students Against Apartheid Coalition 1987b, p. 1105).*

The students appealed, and the Court of Appeals for the Fourth Circuit ruled in favor of the university. The revised policy again was ruled to be content neutral, the interests sought to be protected were the aesthetic interests of maintaining the architectural integrity of part of a national historic landmark, and the regulation was narrowly drawn to prohibit structures only on the south side of the Rotunda (*Students Against Apartheid Coalition* 1988).

This appellate court ruling is important because it is in accord with the U.S. Supreme Court's rejection of the view that the First Amendment protects only literal speech and writings. In *Spence* v. *Washington* (1974), the Supreme Court prohibited the state of Washington from penalizing a defendant for hanging an upside-down American flag with a peace symbol attached to it out his apartment window. The Court articulated two tests for deciding when conduct becomes protected speech: (1) Is the action done with intent to convey a particular message? (2) Does a substantial likelihood exist that the intended audience will understand the action as conveying a message? Thus, in terms of these two tests, the construction of shanties undoubtedly would constitute protected expression. Demonstrators construct them to convey a message, and the campus community understands communication to be their purpose.

Disruptive speech
Students at Auburn University sued their institution for forbidding them to hold a week-long campout at Auburn's designated public forum area, contending that this restriction denied them their constitutional rights. The Student and Fac-

ulty Senate at the university had a policy in effect at the time, "Regulations for Speakers and Demonstrations on the Auburn University Campus," which stated:

> *Auburn University recognizes and supports the rights of students, employees of all categories, and visitors to speak and demonstrate in a lawful manner in designated areas of the campus. In order to maintain campus safety, security, and order, and to insure the orderly scheduling of facilities and to preclude conflicts with academic and co-curricular activities, Auburn University reserves the right to reasonably limit such activities by . . . regulations regarding the time, place, and manner of such activities (Auburn Alliance for Peace and Justice v. Martin 1988, p. 1073).*

The federal district court, like courts in other jurisdictions, determined that Auburn University lawfully had a right to reasonably limit such speech activities by their regulations concerning time, place, and manner of the activities. According to the court, "few would suggest that a university would be forced to allow a speech or a demonstration in the reading room of the library" (p. 1077). In this particular situation, the university had offered to extend the forum's hours and to allow the use of an alternative forum area when the designated area was unavailable. The policies were considered content neutral because they did not relate to the purpose or the content of the campout. Because they granted an absolute right to speak or demonstrate (at the forum area) if no conflicts in scheduling occurred, they were not vague and overbroad.

The courts have agreed that student demonstrations and their related speech activities may be regulated if that speech disrupts normal campus activities or results in substantial disorder on campus. Therefore, reasonable regulations designated for avoiding conflicts in using the designated space, avoiding conflicts with other school activities, and maintaining an atmosphere conducive to the learning environment of the college campus have been upheld as appropriate and lawful. The Supreme Court has defined what constitutes "reasonable" as those restrictions on time, place, and manner "that are without reference to the content of the regulated speech, that . . . are narrowly tailored to serve a significant governmental interest, and that . . . leave open ample alternative channels for communication of the information" (*Clark* v. *Community for Creative Non-Violence* 1984, p. 293).

In conclusion, speech on a college campus in the form of advocacy is entitled to full protection; action is not. College and university administrators therefore have a legitimate interest in preventing disruption on campus, but until actual physical disturbance or disruption occurs, they likewise have a heavy burden to show their justification of any denial of free speech. The Supreme Court in *Healy* recognized the balance between students' rights of free speech and college administrators' corresponding rights for managing their institutions.

> *We . . . hold that a college has the inherent power to promulgate rules and regulations; that it has the inherent power properly to discipline; that it has power appropriately to protect itself and its property; that it may expect that its students adhere to generally accepted standards of conduct* (*Healy* 1972, p. 2352).

MANDATORY DRUG TESTING OF ATHLETES:
The Controversy Continues

Few would argue that drug abuse has become a national concern in the United States. College and university campuses, likewise, have experienced a marked increase in drug use and abuse among students, including destruction and violence against persons and property (U.S. General Accounting Office 1989).

To prevent drug use among athletes, the NCAA has imposed mandatory drug testing at all NCAA championship events in addition to a year-round testing program as a precondition of a student's participation in intercollegiate sports competition (NCAA 1991–92). The NCAA, as well as colleges and universities, has legitimate cause for concern about drug abuse by college students. Mandatory drug testing raises numerous other concerns for college administrators, however. Should student-athletes be treated differently from students who are not athletes? What about students' rights of privacy? Is drug testing accurate? What is the real purpose for testing, and is that purpose met?

Mandatory drug testing raises numerous other concerns for college administrators....

Rights of Privacy
The actual process of testing for drugs is conducted by NCAA staff, who monitor, by observation, the furnishing of the specimen. Students:

> . . . [are] required to disrobe from the area of the armpits to their knees, exposing their genitals, and to produce a urine specimen of at least 100 milliliters while under visual observation. If a subject (student) is unable to "fill the beaker," he or she is given fluids and required to remain under the observation of the NCAA validator until successful (*Hill* v. *NCAA* 1990, p. 405).

Two Stanford University student-athletes, Jennifer Hill, co-captain of the Stanford women's soccer team, and Barry McKeever, a linebacker on the football team, filed a complaint against the NCAA, alleging that its drug testing program violated their rights of privacy guaranteed under the California constitution (*Hill* v. *NCAA* 1988). They contended that the tests were degrading, humiliating, and embarrassing, that the tests were incapable of measuring factors relevant to athletic performance, and that the testing program did not require a showing of individualized suspicion or compelling necessity.

The California court declared the NCAA drug testing program an unconstitutional invasion of privacy because it required the students to reveal potentially sensitive medical information and to be tested while being watched by an NCAA official (*Hill* 1988). The judge issued a permanent injunction exempting Stanford University athletes from the NCAA drug testing program indefinitely. The NCAA appealed, and on September 25, 1990, the California Court of Appeals upheld the trial court's decision on all points and further criticized the NCAA program for its lack of thoroughness in designing its testing program and its doubtful conclusions used to justify the need for a testing program.

The California appellate court ruled that the state constitution provides the guarantee of privacy the status of an inalienable right that reaches to both governmental and nongovernmental conduct, including the action of a private association, such as the NCAA. The court further found that the trial court ruled correctly that (1) the NCAA did not show a compelling interest before invading a fundamental right to privacy; (2) the evidence did not support the NCAA's claim that drug use is significant among college athletes and that, by testing, students' health and safety and integrity of competition would be protected; and (3) the evidence did show that the NCAA testing program was too broad and its accuracy doubtful (*Hill* 1990, pp. 403, 404). Finally, the court found that the NCAA had not adequately considered other, less offensive alternatives to testing.

The California court was the first court of appeals to address drug testing relating to college student-athletes, and, although it applies only to the state of California, the court found the NCAA's policy on urine testing to be inherently intrusive. Whether this ruling will be expanded to other jurisdictions is yet to be determined, but some evidence suggests that it could become reality.

Other Rights under State Constitutions

The Washington constitution, like the California constitution, also contains an explicit reference to a right of privacy. In *O'Halloran* v. *University of Washington* (1988), Elizabeth O'Halloran, a member of the indoor track team, claimed that the university's drug testing program, which permitted testing without individualized reasonable suspicion, constituted an unconstitutional invasion of her privacy as well as unreasonable search and seizure. At trial, the university settled the claim by dropping all mandatory components of its testing program and revising it to require testing only for athletes suspected of drug use. The NCAA joined the suit and was successful in removing the case to the federal court, which concluded that:

> The invasion of O'Halloran's privacy interest by the urine specimen collection procedures was outweighed by the compelling interest of the university and the NCAA in protecting the health of student-athletes, . . . ensuring fair competitions for the student-athletes and the public, and educating about and deterring drug abuse in sports competition (O'Halloran 1988, p. 1007).

The O'Halloran ruling thus validated the constitutionality of public colleges' and universities' drug testing programs that test athletes during their preseason medical examinations. This validation was both short-sighted and short-lived, however, because the ruling was appealed to the Ninth Circuit, which reversed and remanded the case back to the district court with directions for that court to "remand the entire case back to the state court from which it was removed," meaning presumably that an interpretation of the Washington constitution would be a factor in the state court's decision (O'Halloran [9th Cir.] 1988, p. 1381).

Ultimately, the case was settled on the basis that the NCAA issue a public acknowledgment that no evidence existed that student-athlete Elizabeth O'Halloran ever had used drugs and provide her with a transcript of the debate at the 1990 convention on drug testing (Teagarden 1991).

While the judicial reasoning in the O'Halloran ruling appears to be in a different direction from that in the Hill rulings in the California courts, the results were the same in that both final determinations brought the relief sought by the students and, at the same time, forced reversals and corrective actions upon the universities and the NCAA. Further, these rulings confirm that students will take such claims against mandatory drug testing to the state courts of their respective institutions and where the various state statute and constitutional guarantees of privacy and equal protection might apply.

A recent drug testing case in Massachusetts illustrates how judges might respond to such future cases involving private colleges and universities. In this case, *Bally* v. *Northeastern University* (1989), David Bally, a member of Northeastern's varsity indoor track and cross-country teams, refused to sign the school's drug testing consent form as well as the NCAA's drug testing form, actions that made him ineligible for intercollegiate competition. He brought suit against Northeastern, claiming that its policy requiring student-athletes to consent to drug testing as a condition of participating in intercollegiate sports violated his civil rights and his rights of privacy under Massachusetts general law. He did not seek relief from, nor was the NCAA a party to, this case.

Northeastern University answered that the reasons for its testing program were (1) to promote the health and physical safety of student-athletes, (2) to promote fair intrateam and intercollegiate competition, and (3) to ensure that Northeastern student-athletes, as role models for other students and as representatives of Northeastern to the public, are not perceived as drug users (*Bally* 1989, p. 51).

The Superior Court of Suffolk County agreed with David Bally and declared that Northeastern's NCAA-inspired drug testing program violated both the state's Civil Rights Act and Right to Privacy Statute. The university appealed, and the Massachusetts Supreme Court reversed the lower court, stating that the Massachusetts Civil Rights Act was intended to address racial or sexual harassment, not to provide a remedy for individuals like Bally. The court separated Bally's objection to drug testing from those claims for which the court had granted relief in the past, including cases of physical confrontation, sexual harassment, and threats, intimidation, or coercion. Finally, the judge differentiated Bally's claim from previously successful claims on the basis that his did not involve the public disclosure of private information. *Bally* serves to illustrate how private colleges and universities may exercise their broader prerogatives than public institutions in establishing mandatory drug testing programs for their students. The case also demonstrates that, in addition to providing their own privacy statutes, each state may interpret those provisions in whatever manner it chooses. Two states might have identical constitutions, but each might construe its right to privacy in a different way because of different interpretations of the developing case law or because of varying legislative intent when drafting such laws.

Arguments for Testing

The NCAA contends that drug testing protects the health and safety of athletes.

Member institutions are dedicated to the ideal of fair and equitable competition. . . . At the same time . . . so that no one participant might have an artificially induced advantage, so that no one participant might be pressured to use chemical substances . . . to remain competitive, and to safeguard the health and safety of participants, this NCAA drugtesting program has been created (NCAA 1991–92, p. 6).

Colleges and universities also might have specific reasons for wanting drug testing of athletes. Northeastern University, as described earlier, stated that its program is directed toward preventing student-athletes from being perceived as drug users and ensuring that they are role models for other students as well as for the public. Other reasons colleges and universities have given for their mandatory testing programs relate to public policy. The public views institutions of higher education as places that set standards, instill values, and produce future leaders. Thus, a drug testing program for college athletes not only deters the athletes themselves from taking drugs, the reasoning goes, but also serves as a deterrent to other young people who might respect and idolize the athletes (Gibbs 1991). Finally, such policy considerations favor drug testing because it serves as a dynamic and definitive way of delivering drug education information to students as a result of the publicity that generally surrounds student-athletes.

Arguments against Testing

Objections to mandatory drug testing for college athletes range from personal embarrassment at being forced to urinate into a beaker as someone observes to questioning the legitimate interest for testing student-athletes. Athletes and their lawyers have been particularly forceful in their claims that drug testing is a gross invasion of privacy. Not only do athletes find monitored testing embarrassing, they also find it humiliating to be *unable* to urinate as someone observes them (Champion 1991; Leeson 1989; Ranney 1990). In addition, the accuracy of drug tests can be problematic, and NCAA laboratories do not allow for independent confirmation of test results.

The evidence to date shows that the NCAA has had considerable difficulty in demonstrating the legal grounds for its drug testing program. In fact, the NCAA has yet to show the rational relationship of its testing program to valid purposes within its scope as an umbrella organization of amateur sports (Evans 1990; *Dercleyn* v. *University of Colorado* 1991; *Hill* v. *NCAA* 1990).

Does the extent of drug use among student-athletes create a compelling need to test them for drugs? Stanford University said "no," and the *Hill* court agreed. The court concluded that the incidence of drug use among student-athletes is low.

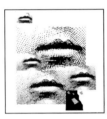

*The NCAA failed to establish that it had a compelling interest in its drug testing program based on evidence of actual use of each of the banned drugs by a significant number of the male and female athletes in each of the 26 NCAA sports (*Hill* 1990, p. 407).*

The court based its conclusions, in part, on data from the 1986–87 NCAA drug tests, which produced only 34 positive tests, less than 1 percent, out of 3,511 students tested. Some might argue, however, that these data do not confirm the absence of a drug problem: Another conclusion could be that some students were deterred from taking drugs because of the tests. Even so, the court could find no legitimate reasons to "single out athletes," because the trial court earlier had found it undisputed that "athletes do not use drugs any more than college students generally or others of their age group, and that they actually use drugs less during the athletic season than their peers" (p. 413).

Federal or State Constitutional Domain?

For student-athletes to challenge successfully that drug testing violates their federal constitutional rights, they must show that it constitutes "state action" and that it deprives them of rights, privileges, or immunities secured by the Constitution. The U.S. Constitution protects against abridgement of individual rights only to the extent that the objectionable conduct is "state action." Thus, a primary question before those courts considering drug testing cases involving the NCAA under federal law has been whether the NCAA is a state actor. In cases involving a university-initiated drug testing program, state colleges and universities are state actors, whereas private institutions are not.

In *NCAA* v. *Tarkanian* (1988), the question was "whether the actions of the University of Nevada–Las Vegas, in compliance with NCAA rules and recommendations, constituted state action" (p. 462). The Supreme Court ruled that, although UNLV without question is a state actor, the NCAA is a private party. This ruling reversed the earlier decision of the Nevada Supreme Court, which had concluded that "the two entities (UNLV and NCAA) had acted jointly to deprive Tarkanian of liberty and property interests, making the NCAA as well as UNLV a state actor" (*NCAA* v. *Tarkanian* 1988, p. 4054).

Although UNLV had some impact on the NCAA's policies, ruled the Supreme Court, such policies also were affected by hundreds of other public and private institutions, most of which were located in states other than Nevada. The NCAA might be more accurately described, therefore, as an agent of its member institutions, which, as competitors of UNLV, hold an interest in the fair enforcement of NCAA's standards of recruitment.

Rules promulgated by the NCAA and their enforcement thus constitute private conduct, not state action, and, in light of the *Tarkanian* ruling, it appears questionable whether any student-athlete will challenge successfully that the NCAA's drug testing program violates the Constitution. Students who object to mandatory drug testing will most likely register their legal claims in their respective institutions' state courts rather than the federal court system.

In the meantime, and until the courts are more consistent and more specific, certain indicators exist as to appropriate "safeguards" for colleges and universities to follow in designing policies and in implementing those policies for drug testing programs. The following examples illustrate the courts' primary concerns.

NCAA or institution?

Colleges and universities cannot hide behind the NCAA's "requirement" of drug testing by claiming that they are not involved directly, that testing is one of the NCAA's rules. It is correct that the NCAA's rules and regulations apply directly to student-athletes both on and off the field, but it is not the NCAA that directly disciplines students; it is the institution. NCAA member institutions are required to "apply and enforce

NCAA legislation against student-athletes on pain of discipline, including suspension from participation in intercollegiate games and expulsion" (*Hill* 1990, p. 405). Therefore, both institution and NCAA are directly involved, even when the testing program has been dictated by the NCAA.

NCAA member colleges and universities must enforce the policies against the student-athlete or be vulnerable to NCAA sanctions. The institution thus finds itself between the NCAA and the student. Does it yield to NCAA and go against its student in court, or does it join the student and go to court against the NCAA? Either choice involves time-consuming activities and costly legal fees as well as public relations problems. Colleges and universities might decide it unwise to delegate these matters to the NCAA and instead conduct their own drug testing programs and drug education activities (Evans 1990). NCAA member institutions likewise have the collective authority to change or curtail NCAA policies. Whatever actions an institution takes, one of its most important considerations is to develop clear and definitive policy objectives for institutional drug testing programs and match the program content and testing procedures to achieve the desired outcome.

Importance of drug education
The *Hill* court (1990) was concerned that the NCAA did not have a drug education program, emphasizing that "the NCAA does not provide any counseling [or] rehabilitation, or offer schools or universities any assistance in counseling or rehabilitation for athletes who are found to have a drug problem under the drug testing program" (p. 418). Moreover, the NCAA's program was declared illegal because it had not adequately attempted drug education as an appropriate alternative to drug testing. The NCAA's own survey showed that, in the first year of the drug testing program, 75 percent of the schools did not have a plan for treating athletes found to have problems with drug dependency and that, in the second year, nearly 60 percent of the schools still did not have rehabilitation plans (*Hill* 1990, p. 418).

Some educators contend that education alone is not sufficient to combat substance abuse, but a substantial consensus appears to exist that drug education can be effective in the prevention as well as in the treatment and rehabilitation of individuals who have been substance abusers. The NCAA now has initiated programs in the prevention of drug use, in intervention, and in education "that reach out to college student-athletes, coaches, and athletics administrators, as well as to grade-school and high school youth" (NCAA 1991–92, p. 2). Although it will take time to show the validity of these activities and to determine whether they are seriously intended, evidence of their high priority and visibility in the NCAA could be critical in curtailing drug abuse in collegiate athletics.

If colleges and universities are serious about addressing drug abuse among students, they should have their own drug education programs for all their students, including athletes. Numerous experts maintain that alcohol constitutes the most serious substance abuse problem among college and university students, and to date neither the NCAA nor higher education institutions comprehensively and adequately include alcohol in their drug testing programs or their drug education activities.

The accuracy of testing
Many judges involved with litigation regarding drug testing during the past several years have expressed considerable concern and dismay over the errors, inaccurate results, and inconsistent findings in drug tests. For example, on October 11, 1991, Judge Douglas Harkin ruled against the NCAA and the University of Montana and for student-athlete Steve Premock because the NCAA's drug testing samples were not handled properly at the laboratory where the samples were analyzed (*NCAA News* 1991, p. 1). Premock had been declared ineligible pursuant to the NCAA's testing rules, but the judge concluded that "no credible evidence has been presented to indicate that Steve Premock is a steroid drug user" (p. 12).

The *Hill* court discovered that it is possible for athletes to test positive just by passively inhaling marijuana smoke in a room. In addition, NCAA drug testing does not test impairment at the point of testing; instead, it measures the history of drug use (Champion 1991, p. 272). Thus, it is possible that a positive test could result from a drug ingested months before the actual testing.

Do better alternatives exist for accuracy and timing of tests? Institutions must make every effort to document that their testing programs address these concerns in the most effective manner. Blood tests, for example, might be considered rather than urinalysis, or students might be given a choice of testing methods. Whatever the approach, institutions should inform incoming athletes well in advance of their anticipated enrollment that the institution and/or the NCAA may test them for drugs.

Because the accuracy of tests is limited, procedural safeguards should be incorporated in any drug testing program to allow students who test positive to respond to or rebut the findings. Such students should be allowed access to an additional analysis by an independent laboratory.

Issues of privacy

The *Bally* ruling is the only reported instance involving drug testing of college student-athletes in which institutional monitoring of the athletes' act of urination was upheld. The court reached this conclusion because it considered monitoring the only means of ensuring that the athlete submits his or her own urine to be tested, as drug-free urine is commercially available and, without a monitor, might be substituted for the athlete's urine. Most courts agree, however, that one's urine is not subject to public examination and that a legitimate expectation of privacy does exist for college athletes (*McDonnell* v. *Hunter* 1984).

> *One does not reasonably expect to discharge urine under circumstances making it available to others to collect and analyze in order to discover the personal secrets it holds* (p. 1127).

Although the Supreme Court has not addressed directly the monitoring of athletes' urination, it has upheld the requiring of urine and blood samples, *minus* monitoring, from Federal Railroad Administration employees involved in accidents and violations of safety rules. The nation's highest court ruled that these testing requirements did not unconstitutionally invade the privacy of the employees involved in accidents and the violation of safety rules, as "the regulations did not require that samples be furnished under direct observation of a monitor despite a desirability of the procedure to ensure integrity of sample, and that sample was collected in medical environment" (*Skinner* v. *Railway Labor Executives' Association* 1989, p. 1404).

College athletes neither are federal employees nor charged with the responsibility for travelers' safety on a nationwide

railway system. It would seem appropriate, therefore, that
should colleges and universities continue the use of urinalysis,
the collection procedures need not include monitoring. Drug
testers could continue to frisk athletes but then allow them
time to urinate privately in an appropriately and systematically
checked booth. Dye in the toilet bowls could be used to prevent students from substituting water for the sample, and the
observer standing outside the booth could check the temperature of the sample, by hand, to ensure its genuineness
(*Schaill by Kross* v. *Tippecanoe County School Corporation*
1988).

Consent
Although courts in various jurisdictions have not reached the
same conclusions on the legal and educational boundaries
of drug testing, they agree that the relationship between a college and its athletes is contractual if the student offers athletic
services in exchange for something, typically a scholarship
or grant. If students verify their intent to enroll at an NCAA
member institution through a National Letter of Intent, for
example, they negotiate it in exchange for financial aid.

Under such a contractual relationship, if students should
also sign an Advance Consent form to be tested for drugs at
some unidentified future time, it would be considered a valid
contract if no duress, undue influence, or grossly one-sided
elements had been involved in the decision to sign the contract (Pernell 1990). Some might argue that student-athletes
would be under duress, or even coercion, as they would not
receive financial aid or be allowed to participate in the
school's athletic program if they did not sign the contract.
Conversely, it might be argued that the failure to sign an
Advance Consent form to be tested for drugs does not prevent
students' admission to the institution and receiving financial
aid of another form. Students would not be denied a college
education simply by failing to sign the form and thereby not
participating in athletics. This dilemma certainly presents a
difficult choice, but it is not one in which duress or undue
influence could be easily documented.

Nonetheless, colleges and universities, their coaches and
representatives, and even currently enrolled student-athletes
should exercise extreme care that any written or verbal communication or any behavior on their part not infringe on the
recruited student's free will to enter into a contractual agree-

*. . . procedural
safeguards
should be
incorporated
in any drug
testing
program to
allow students
who test
positive to
respond to or
rebut the
findings.*

ment, infringe on the superior position of the college or university to force subservient students to sign such a document, or infringe in a manner that courts could deem unconscionable, whereby students realistically have no choice but to sign an agreement or contract.

Compelling need

The Colorado Court of Appeals, on December 19, 1991, upheld a lower court's ruling that prohibited the University of Colorado at Boulder from conducting mandatory drug testing of its student-athletes (*Dercleyn* v. *University of Colorado* 1991). The court ruled that the university's random drug testing program violated the protection of privacy of both the Colorado and U.S. constitutions and that it could conduct mandatory testing only if it showed a "compelling state need" to do so.

The reasoning of the Colorado Appeals Court is similar to that used by the California Court of Appeals in *Hill* (1990) in that both courts found failures to show a compelling need to test student-athletes, thereby treating them differently from other students. The University of Colorado did not document or show a reasonable justification for testing athletes, just as the NCAA failed to show that its need to test outweighed any resulting impairment of a constitutional right. The NCAA contended that it had two compelling reasons for its drug testing program: first, to protect the health and safety of student-athletes and, second, to preserve fair and equitable competition. The court determined, however, that neither reason had merit. It found "no evidence that drug use in athletic competition was endangering the health and safety of student-athletes" (*Hill* 1990, p. 417), and it concluded that none of the drugs on the NCAA banned list would actually enhance the performance of those individuals participating in NCAA sports.

The Colorado Court of Appeals defined "compelling need," in part, by whether a "reasonable suspicion" was involved that would, in the court's view, justify a compelling reason to test athletes for drugs. The American Civil Liberties Union, however, contends that random drug testing still would not be justifiable because "reasonable suspicion" leads to the conclusion that unless the university "witnesses evidence of drug use, or has good circumstantial evidence . . . it simply will not be able to meet that standard" (*Chronicle of Higher Education* 1992a, p. A36).

Summary

It is evident that many colleges and universities continue to find themselves embroiled in controversy with their students, the NCAA, or both, over testing student-athletes for drugs. Reconciling the rights and responsibilities of the institution while safeguarding the rights of student-athletes has been no easy task: Some courts have been in agreement while others have reached different conclusions. Even so, the issues are now well defined, and the colleges and universities best able to defend themselves and their drug testing programs have done so when they could show that their policies were designed for a significant compelling reason, that the implementation of the policies accomplishes their designed purpose, that the policies and their implementation specifically accommodate their respective state constitutional requirements of privacy and equal protection, and that they conform to due process in all matters, but particularly testing procedures, accuracy of the tests, and verification of test results.

It is also clear from the legal rulings to date that the joint involvement of the NCAA and its member institutions in drug testing programs for student-athletes could create additional problems for the institution. Colleges and universities should therefore be careful to define their respective prerogatives in such drug testing programs, whether the programs are institutionally sponsored or jointly sponsored with the NCAA.

COLLEGES' EXPOSURE TO LIABILITY:
Students' Safety and Security

Campus crime is not a new development, but on many campuses today, crime has moved from a minor disturbance to a major concern. In fact, evidence indicates that the rate of crime on campuses is nearly the same as in society at large (McEvoy 1992). College campuses are no longer sanctuaries or Ivory Towers isolated from other people. They are now part of modern society, and today's college students represent the general population, including its cultural, social, ethnic, and religious diversity.

It is thus not surprising that crime, sometimes at its worst, has come to campus; the primary problem is how to deal with it. Colleges and universities can educate their students in ways to avoid and prevent crimes as well as ways to protect themselves. Such educational programs and activities are extremely important for both students and institutions, but they are rarely sufficient. Injuries or acts of crime to students do not often end with the victim. Injured students, their parents, a spouse, or their families continue to initiate negligence suits by asking the courts to hold colleges responsible for the safety and security of students and to protect them from harm.

Students who sue colleges and universities for the harm to them resulting from violent crime or injuries sustained on campus generally claim that such harm is the result of the institution's negligence. To prove the college's or university's negligence—and therefore liability—students must first establish that the college or university owed them a duty of care, that a breach of the duty caused them to suffer harm, and that the institution's conduct or lack of conduct was the proximate cause of the harm that resulted in actual loss or injury (Keeton 1984). The key for determining negligence rests on whether a duty of care exists.

The following legal rulings provide considerable insight as to how and under what circumstances the nation's courts are holding colleges and universities liable for the safety and security of their students.

Liability for Sexual Attacks on Students
Two leading cases serve to illustrate when and under what conditions colleges may be held liable for on-campus attacks on their students: *Mullins* v. *Pine Manor College* (1983) and *Miller* v. *State of New York* (1985).

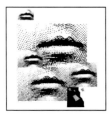

In *Mullins,* a female student at Pine Manor College was raped on campus by a male intruder, never identified, who entered her residence hall room in the early morning hours. He placed a pillowcase over her head, led her out of the building, across the campus into the refectory building through an unlocked door, back outside, then into the refectory again, where he raped her. The episode lasted 60 to 90 minutes, and they were outside on the campus for at least 20 minutes.

Pine Manor is located in an area with relatively few reports of violent crime at the time of the attack, although it is also located a short distance from bus and subway lines going directly to Boston. The campus was surrounded by a six-foot-high chain fence, and the gates were locked between 5 P.M. and 7 A.M. Two guards were on duty, one at the main entrance and one assigned to patrol the campus. Students entered their residence halls after entering through the main gate with their own keys during the evening and night.

The Massachusetts Supreme Court held the college liable for the attack on Lisa Mullins.

> *The fact that a college need not police the morals of its residence students does not entitle it to abandon any effort to ensure their physical safety. Parents, students, and the general community still have a reasonable expectation, fostered in part by colleges themselves, that reasonable care will be exercised to protect resident students from foreseeable harm (Mullins 1983, p. 335).*

The court determined that the attack and rape on campus were foreseeable. Students had been warned during freshman orientation of the dangers inherent in living near a metropolitan area and near bus and train lines. According to the court, such warnings and precautions taken by the college to protect their students against criminal acts of third parties revealed that the school actually had foreseen risk. The *Mullins* ruling is important because the court recognized the student's right to rely on the college's duty, or voluntary undertaking, to protect her security and safety. It is an established principle that "a duty voluntarily assumed must be performed with due care" (*Mullins* 1983, p. 331).

The second prominent case involving sexual assaults on campus denotes that once the college is on notice of the likelihood of criminal harm because of a history of criminal incidents (risk is thus "foreseeable"), the institution has not only a duty to warn, as during the orientation program at Pine Manor College, but also a duty to use due care to adequately protect its students. In *Miller* v. *State of New York* (1985), Madelyn Miller, a junior at the State University of New York at Stony Brook, was confronted in the laundry room of her residence hall at 6 o'clock in the morning by a man wielding a large butcher knife. She was blindfolded and taken out of the room, through an unlocked outer door from the basement, back in another unlocked entrance to the dormitory, up some stairs to the third floor, and into a dormitory room, where she was raped twice at knifepoint and threatened with mutilation or death if she made any noise. Her assailant finally abandoned her and was never identified.

The trial court found that he was an intruder with no right to be there. There had been reports to campus security of strangers in the hallways and of men present in a women's bathroom. The court awarded $25,000 for emotional injuries to the student because of the university's negligence. The New York Court of Appeals ruled that when the state operates housing, it is held to the same duty as private landlords in the maintenance of physical security. The student in this case therefore could hold the institution liable by showing that a reasonably foreseeable likelihood of criminal intrusion into the building was present, that the university negligently failed to keep outer doors locked, and that such failure was proximate cause of the injury (*Miller* 1984, p. 830).

In this situation, the student was successful in her claim because the institution failed to meet its responsibilities in the landlord/tenant relationship. A special relationship existed between the student and her university, and the institution's failure to lock the outer doors of the dormitory was a breach of duty as well as a proximate cause of the rape.

As a landowner, the state must act as a reasonable [person] in maintaining his property in a reasonably safe condition in view of all the circumstances, including the likelihood of injury to others, the seriousness of the injury, and the burden of avoiding the risk. Under this standard, a landlord has a duty to maintain minimal security measures related to a specific building, itself, in the face of foreseeable criminal intrusion upon tenants (Miller 1984, p. 833).

The New York State Supreme Court held that the earlier $25,000 award for damages was inadequate and that "considering the horror of the rape itself and the consequences that followed, an award of $400,000 is in order" (*Miller* 1985, p. 116).

In both *Mullins* and *Miller,* the colleges were held to a standard of reasonable care and were held liable because harm to students had been foreseeable. The courts also determined that in these episodes the colleges had not used due care in providing adequate security protection. Such rulings are common, and the element of foreseeability has become the criterion for determining an institution's liability for criminal attacks on its students.

The Principle of Business/Invitee

In *Peterson* v. *San Francisco Community College District* (1984), the court held the college liable for a sexual attack on a student that occurred in the college parking lot. An unidentified man jumped from behind "unreasonably thick and untrimmed foliage and trees" adjoining the stairway and attempted to rape her. The college was aware that other assaults of a similar nature had occurred in the area and had taken some steps to protect students who used the parking lot and stairway. It had not publicized prior incidents or in any way warned the student that she was in danger of being attacked in that area of campus, however.

Liability in this situation was based on the college's duty to provide safe premises through exercising due care. The college was responsible for the same standards on which general liability of a landowner for its premises is based, although the ruling held the college to a slightly higher standard than the typical landowner, emphasizing that the college was responsible for overseeing its campus.

The *Peterson* court based its analysis on the existence of a special relationship between the parties that gave rise to a duty of care. The special relationship the court explicitly pointed to was the one "between a possessor of land and members of the public who enter in response to the landowner's invitation" (*Peterson* 1984, p. 1196). It is clear from the language in the *Peterson* ruling that something is even more special about the relationship between student and college that serves as the basis for liability:

In the enclosed environment of a school campus where students pay tuition and other fees in exchange for using the facilities, where they spend a significant portion of their time and may in fact live, they can reasonably expect that the premises will be free from physical defects and that school authorities will also exercise reasonable care to keep the campus free from conditions [that] increase the risk of crime (Peterson 1984, p. 1201).

The duty of due care includes a duty to warn students of a foreseeable injury so that they can take necessary action to protect themselves. If a college or university does not meet the standard of due care, it can be held liable. The circumstances in the *Peterson* litigation were clear: The college knew of the dangers in the dark parking lot and had not cut foliage that had grown and blocked the stairway to the parking lot. In addition, the college had not warned the student in any way of the inherent danger.

In a similar situation but with a different outcome, two female undergraduate students at Florida Atlantic University were assaulted, abducted by three men, and murdered. The court refused to hold the university liable, however, because no evidence existed of serious crimes against anyone on campus since the university opened in 1963. The criminal activity was therefore *not* foreseeable, and thus no duty to protect the student was present (*Relyea* v. *State of Florida* 1980). The North Carolina Court of Appeals used the same approach and reached the same conclusion in *Brown* v. *North Carolina Wesleyan College* (1983), a case involving a college cheerleader who was abducted from a basketball game, raped, and murdered. The court relied on the concept of foreseeability to determine whether the college had a duty to protect its students from such criminal acts. Wesleyan College had experienced only scattered vandalism and break-ins and one attempted rape two years before this incident. Because of these circumstances, the court concluded that insufficient reason existed to impose a duty upon the college to safeguard its students from criminal assaults (*Brown* 1983).

These cases illustrate that, as a matter of principle, when students sue their colleges and show that their relationship to their institution is that of a landowner or business and invitee, a duty to warn or protect arises when the criminal activity of a third person is "reasonably foreseeable." In these situations, such foreseeability is present if the college or university has prior knowledge of similar criminal behavior on its campus. It is this foreseeability that creates the duty to warn students of potential harm and to exercise reasonable care in ensuring their physical safety. Colleges and universities must show that they use due care and that they do not abandon efforts to maintain safe premises.

Injuries to Students Not Involving Assaults

Injuries to students on campus are obviously not always the result of criminal attacks. Moreover, numerous injuries to students involve no other individual but result from the student's own carelessness or the institution's failure to meet adequate responsibilities for safety and security. It is these types of injuries, or alleged injuries, that too often can lead to legal claims against the college or university for the harm the student suffered.

An example of such an injury is the case where a student filed suit against his university for injuries he suffered when he fell on a patch of ice on the school's parking lot. In *Russell* v. *Board of Regents of University of Nebraska* (1988), the student was walking from a classroom building to his car when he fell and fractured his ankle. The Nebraska Supreme Court ruled that the trial court was correct in determining that the university had been negligent in the creation of a dangerous condition by placing a pile of snow in such a position that normal temperature changes would cause the snow to melt, that it would refreeze during the night's lower temperatures, and that the result would be the formation of ice on the parking lot. The court concluded further that the danger presented by the ice was not obvious to the student and that the student had used ordinary care (*Russell* 1988).

In this situation, the danger of the harm was foreseeable by the university. The maintenance people knew, or should have known, according to the court, that the typical higher temperatures of the day would melt some of the snow and that the subfreezing temperatures of the early morning hours would cause the water from melting snow to refreeze. Despite this knowledge, the university "failed to put any deicing material [on the parking lot] . . . where the plaintiff fell . . . [although it] had ample time to do so" (*Russell* 1988, p. 128). The injured student was an "invitee" in the sense that he could reasonably expect his college's parking lot to be safe. It was not safe, and the fault had not been his as he had *not* contributed to his own injury.

While this particular student was awarded $21,000 for his injury, not a large award by some standards, it is safe to assume that had the harm been greater, the institutional liability also would have been greater.

Another case involving injury to a student but with a different conclusion was brought to the courts by Jeffrey Furek, a fraternity pledge who was burned when lye-based liquid oven cleaner was poured over his body during fraternity hazing (*Furek* v. *University of Delaware* 1991). The jury awarded Furek damages of $30,000 against the university and the fraternity member involved in the incident. Upon appeal and cross appeal, the Delaware Supreme Court found that the university "could be held liable for breach of duty of supervision and protection under the circumstances" (*Furek* 1991, p. 506). These circumstances, according to the court, were that the university not only was knowledgeable of the dangers of hazing, but also, in repeated communications with students in general and fraternity members in particular, had emphasized the university's policy of discipline for hazing infractions. The state supreme court found that:

> . . . the University's policy against hazing, like its overall commitment to provide security on its campus, thus constituted an assumed duty, which became an indispensable part of the bundle of services [that] colleges afford their students (*Furek* 1991, p. 520, quoting *Mullins* 1983, p. 336).

Even so, the court emphasized, "The magnitude of the burden placed on the university is no greater than to require compliance with self-imposed standards" (*Furek* 1991, p. 523). The primary fault in this case was the university's failure to exercise greater control over a known hazardous activity—hazing. The court concluded, however, that the university's actions, while ineffectual, were well-intentioned and not characterized by a conscious disregard to a known risk. The university, under the circumstances, did have *some* duty of supervision and protection for Furek's safety, but the court stopped short of finding the relationship between university and student sufficiently strong to entitle the student to recover punitive damages from his institution.

Furek serves as a warning to college and university administrators that future courts could require more, not less, direct supervision for student organizations and activities.

> *The university is not an insurer of the safety of its students, nor a policeman of student morality[;] nonetheless, it has a duty to regulate and supervise foreseeable dangerous activities occurring on its property. That duty extends to the negligent or intentional activities of third persons (Furek 1991, p. 522).*

One of the most important cases involving injury to a student in which the college was found not liable is *Whitlock* v. *University of Denver* (1987), which involved a claim by sophomore Oscar Whitlock for paralyzing injuries he sustained in a trampoline accident at his fraternity house. Whitlock had been jumping on the trampoline all afternoon, and he was still jumping on it that evening, during a fraternity party, when he landed on his head and was rendered a quadriplegic.

The Colorado district court determined that Whitlock had been 28 percent negligent and assigned the University of Denver 72 percent of the causal negligence. It awarded $5,256,000 to Whitlock against the university, but the appeals court reversed the ruling, placing an even greater legal duty on the university. Finally, after seven years of litigation, the Colorado Supreme Court struck down the earlier rulings, mandating that:

> *. . . the university did not owe a duty of care to the student to take reasonable measures to protect him against injuries resulting from his use of trampoline, which was owned by fraternity and was located on the front lawn of the house that fraternity leased from university (Whitlock 1987, p. 54).*

The facts of the case indicated that the relationship between student and university was not sufficiently special to impose upon the institution a duty to protect fraternity members from the dangers of social activities in general and trampoline jumping in particular. The relationship was not one of dependence, it was not one of landlord/tenant, the student was not an "invitee" as in *Peterson* and *Russell,* and the University of Denver had not shown, either by policy or action, that it had assumed responsibility for the social and recreational activities of the fraternity members. There was therefore "no basis for the recognition of a duty of the university to take measures for protection of Whitlock against the injury that he suffered" (*Whitlock* 1987, p. 61).

Alcohol-Related Injuries

Courts generally have refused to hold colleges liable for injuries to students resulting from the misuse of alcohol. In numerous jurisdictions involving a variety of alcohol-related suits against institutions, it appears that state courts are taking a hands-off position by their inconsistencies in case analysis and by their apparent acceptance of the fact that college students are going to drink, just as people drink in society in general. Even so, some of the legal boundaries of liability are implicit in several court decisions.

The leading case in this area is *Bradshaw* v. *Rawlings* (1979), in which Donald Bradshaw, a sophomore at Delaware Valley College, was injured in an automobile accident following an off-campus picnic sponsored by the sophomore class. He was a passenger in a car driven by another student, and both had been drinking at the picnic. A faculty member who served as sophomore class adviser had assisted in planning the picnic and had co-signed a check for class funds that was used to purchase beer. The picnic was an annual event for the sophomore class, and flyers announcing the picnic were displayed prominently across campus. The legal drinking age in the state was 21, but the majority of the students drinking at the picnic were 19- and 20-year-old sophomores.

In rejecting the student's claim that the college had a duty to protect his safety at this college-sponsored and -financed event, the court responded that "the modern American college is not an insurer of the safety of its students" (*Bradshaw* 1979, p. 138).

By constitutional amendment, written and unwritten law, and through the evolution of new customs, rights formerly possessed by college administrations have been transferred to students. College students today are no longer minors; they are now regarded as adults in almost every phase of community life.... [E]xcept for purchasing alcoholic beverages, eighteen year old persons are considered adults by

Courts generally have refused to hold colleges liable for injuries to students resulting from the misuse of alcohol.

the Commonwealth of Pennsylvania (Bradshaw 1979,
p. 139).

The court contended that students are independent from,
rather than dependent upon, the colleges and universities
they attend. If no special relationship exists, liability cannot
be attached. The court reasoned further that college students'
drinking beer is a common activity and in and of itself is not
dangerous. Thus, according to such an analysis, Donald Bradshaw's injury was not foreseeable. This ruling must be limited
to its specific facts, but it has served as legal precedent in
numerous subsequent rulings that colleges do not owe students a duty of care when it comes to their own reckless use
of alcohol.

In a similar case but seven years after *Bradshaw,* a 20-year-
old student at the University of Utah suffered quadriplegia
following a university-sponsored biology field trip, when she
wandered from the campsite and fell off a cliff (*Beach* v. *University of Utah* 1986). She and other students, as well as the
professor, had been drinking before the accident. The Utah
Supreme Court ruled that:

> *Colleges and universities are educational institutions, not
> custodial. . . . It would be unrealistic to impose upon an
> institution of higher education the additional role of cus-
> todian over its adult students and to charge it with respon-
> sibility for preventing students from illegally consuming
> alcohol and, should they do so, with the responsibility for
> assuring their safety and the safety of others. . . . Fulfilling
> this charge would require the institution to babysit each stu-
> dent, a task beyond the resources of any school* (*Beach* 1986,
> p. 419).

One of the most recent rulings, a 1991 California Court of
Appeals action, involved a female student who was raped in
a University of California–Berkeley dormitory after a party at
which alcohol had been served to students under 21 years
of age (*Tanja H.* v. *Regents of the University of California*
1991). The trial court dismissed the student's claims against
the university and its officials, stating that the university was
not liable to the student. The student appealed, contending
that alcohol had been served in the dormitory to underage
students and that the four perpetrators, all members of the

university football team, were so much bigger, heavier, and stronger than she that she had feared for her safety if she did not comply with their demands.

The Court of Appeals, while acknowledging the outrageous and reprehensible conduct of the perpetrators, upheld the trial court's action in dismissing the claim, finding that the university's safety and security measures in the dormitory, or lack thereof, had not been the cause of the rape. In addition, the court concluded that "universities are not generally liable for the sometimes disastrous consequences [that] result from combining young students, alcohol, and dangerous or violent impulses" (*Tanja H.* 1991, p. 920).

Such rulings support the proposition that alcohol consumption falls outside the scope of the relationship between college and student; therefore, no duty of care and no liability exist on the part of the college or university. Accordingly, it appears that when colleges can show that students can protect themselves better than the colleges and when students' own negligence causes their injuries, no liability will be attached to the institutions, at least in alcohol-related injuries.

Colleges and universities can best defend themselves before the courts from charges stemming from students' alcohol-related injuries by showing that they enforce state and local laws pertaining to alcohol purchase and use and that they provide educational programs to students and student groups concerning the use and abuse of alcohol.

The Relationship between College and Student
These contemporary personal injury cases brought by students against their colleges employ the concept of negligence in their arguments that colleges should be held liable for their injuries. In all of these cases, courts have used a common thread of analysis, holding that a special relationship between the plaintiff student and the defendant college or university must be present to create a duty, the breach of which causes liability to attach. For example, in *Peterson,* the court found that:

> *A duty may arise . . . where (a) a special relation exists between the actor and the third person [that] imposes a duty upon the actor to control the third person's conduct, or (b) a special relation exists between the actor and the other [that] gives the other a right to protection (Peterson 1984, p. 1196).*

In *Miller,* the relationship between the student and university was determined to be that of a private landlord. The institution therefore had a duty, just as a landlord, to maintain its property in a reasonably safe condition, including a likelihood of injury to others. In this case, the institution failed to show that it had fulfilled that duty, and the court ruled that it was liable for its negligence.

Russell is an example of still another court's using the same thread of analysis to determine whether a duty was present, and that court found the relationship between the student and his institution to be that of "invitee," just as the *Peterson* court had done. The student was using the parking lot at his university in the normal way one would use such a facility to attend classes. In fact, the parking lot was there for that specific purpose. Reasonable care, however, had not been taken to make the area safe following a snow storm. The institution's duty to "provide ordinary care and prudence to avoid danger" had not been met, and it was that failure that constituted negligence (*Russell* 1988, p. 128).

Until the 1960s, the relationship between a college and its students was somewhat like that between a parent and child. Indeed, for all practical purposes, the college stood in loco parentis and was the de facto and de jure guardian of students' morals, health, welfare, and safety. The cultural revolution of the late 1960s, however, witnessed the emerging of college and university students' new independence. In the wake of student protests against the Vietnam war and against racial and gender inequality, society began to perceive the college student as an adult rather than a child. Further, the ratification in 1971 of the 26th Amendment to the Constitution, which lowered the federal voting age to 18, provided even more rationale for a new arms-length relationship between colleges and their students. Not only students but also society in general and courts in particular viewed the older, parental relationship as inappropriate (Richmond 1990a; *Beach* 1986; *Bradshaw* 1979).

The Ohio Court of Common Pleas stated a new societal view of the relationship between college and student:

A university is an institution for the advancement of knowledge and learning. It is neither a nursery school, a boarding school, nor a prison. No one is required to attend. Persons who meet the required qualifications and who abide by the

university's rules and regulations are permitted to attend
and must be presumed to have sufficient maturity to con-
duct their own personal affairs (Hegel v. Langsam 1971,
p. 357).

College students therefore possessed newfound freedoms,
a status that also brought a corollary new freedom for their
institutions in that they no longer were held liable under the
in loco parentis relationship for injuries sustained by students.
But students wanted the best of both worlds. While they
demanded their autonomy as adults, they "still expected the
college to protect them from themselves and the actions of
others" (Bhirdo 1989, p. 122). As these legal cases disclose,
students injured on campus or in campus-related activities
continue to sue their institutions for negligence. The courts,
moreover, continue to struggle with defining the "special"
relationship between colleges and their students.

Defenses against Negligence

Colleges and universities have used four primary categories
of defense in meeting charges of institutional negligence: contributory negligence, comparative negligence, assumption
of risk, and immunity.

Contributory negligence is used when the harm suffered
can be partly or wholly attributable to the student's own negligence. In states that recognize contributory negligence, the
institution must show that the students failed to exercise ordinary care, that they failed to follow instructions, or that they
in some way were responsible for their own injuries. In jurisdictions citing strict contributory negligence, if an injured student is negligent and that negligence contributes to his or
her harm, then the defendant college or university that is also
negligent may be absolved from liability. When the plaintiff
students' fault contributes to their injury, they are prevented
from recovering any damages at all. Some courts have held
that complete barring of all damages because of contributory
fault is too extreme, and they therefore have attempted to prorate damages for comparative negligence. In states with statutes covering comparative negligence, the plaintiffs, even
though themselves partly to blame for their own harm, will
not be totally barred from recovery.

Assumption of risk is used when the institution can show
that the injured student knew of the danger involved and vol-

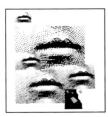

untarily chose to accept the risk. If a student is ignorant of the danger, however, he or she does not assume the risk.

Whitlock (1987) illustrates both comparative negligence and assumption of risk. Oscar Whitlock, the student who suffered quadriplegia resulting from his falling off the trampoline, testified that he was aware of the risk of an accident and injury of the very nature he sustained. Further, the University of Denver was able to show the court that Whitlock's own negligence had contributed to his injury. The court found, in fact, that Whitlock had been 28 percent negligent and assigned 72 percent of causal negligence to the university. As the case actually concluded, after nine years, Whitlock's claim of negligence failed because the relationship between student and university was not "sufficiently special" to create a duty for the university to protect the student from injuries (*Whitlock* 1987, p. 54). Moreover, the university had been successful in using both these defenses throughout the entire litigation.

Colleges and universities use governmental immunity as a defense against negligence in some states, but this defense has, for the most part, eroded. In the states where it survives in one form or another, it applies only to public, or tax-assisted, institutions, not privately supported colleges and universities. Charitable immunity, which privately supported colleges and universities have used in some states as a defense against negligence, also has eroded during recent years, and the trend is toward treating a charity like any other business organization.

Summary

In situations involving the victimization of students as well as other personal injuries to students on campus, the element of foreseeability has become a criterion in many states for determining colleges' and universities' liability. For example, the extent to which an institution knew, or should have known, that a student was exposed, or could be exposed, to a risk of injury is a major factor in courts' determining whether the institution owed a duty of care to the student. In cases involving liability for crime on campus, in particular, the courts in numerous jurisdictions have acknowledged the dependent status of students in relation to their colleges. They have used concepts of landlord/tenant and business/invitee, among others, to designate the relationship between college and student. If the relationship between college and student is "sufficiently special," it appears that courts are willing to hold institutions to a duty of care, particularly if the harm is reasonably foreseeable. Actions that are "not reasonably foreseeable and . . . cannot be reasonably anticipated do not result in liability," however (Brown 1990, p. 2).

CONCLUSIONS AND RECOMMENDATIONS FOR POLICY AND PRACTICE

This volume focuses on the complexities involved in reconciling rights and responsibilities between higher education institutions and their students. The courts have been definitive that students do not leave their constitutional rights at the schoolhouse door when they enter colleges and universities. At the same time, however, colleges and universities have rights and responsibilities for maintaining an educational environment conducive for *all* students to learn, to benefit from those same constitutional prerogatives that apply to all citizens, and to be reasonably safe from unlawful activity. Perhaps too often, the educational priorities of colleges and universities and the individual rights of students have come into conflict with each other.

Offensive Speech on Campus

To date, U.S. courts have not looked favorably at colleges' and universities' administrative policies designed to regulate speech, even offensive or hate speech. A prohibition of speech, by whatever definition, places colleges and universities in the position of determining which speech is deemed worthy and which is not, and it is this attempt to regulate expression on the basis of its message or content, or on the basis of selected categories, that courts have held to be in violation of the First Amendment.

Institutional officials considering the adoption of policies to proscribe speech on state college or university campuses might find it helpful to consider the rulings of those courts that have responded to policies regulating speech. Several guiding principles have emerged from recent case law.

- Speech or expression may not be punished on the basis of the subjects the speech addresses. The government must be neutral when it regulates speech.
- Overbroad policies regulating speech have been ruled unconstitutional.
- Unduly vague policies regulating speech have been ruled unconstitutional.
- Restrictions on time, place, and manner of speech or expression appropriate for the educational environment and for maintaining order on campus are constitutional.
- Policy based on "fighting words," even in part, cannot discriminate on the basis of content or viewpoint.

• Policies and procedures addressing due process should be in place before and followed during any disciplinary process.

Privately supported colleges and universities, although not generally under constitutional mandates, might find it desirable to weigh the merits of providing the same rights to their students as public institutions. In addition to contractual considerations, privately supported colleges and universities still must deal with issues of "self" respect, students' expectations, and image, among others.

Considerable consensus exists in the literature that, even if policies restricting speech could be narrowly drawn to be considered lawful by the courts, they do not adequately address the root causes of racism, sexism, or other forms of harassment. Numerous educators have argued that education is the better route to destroying prejudice and bigotry—not regulations, codes, and discipline. In fact, rules prohibiting offensive remarks, slurs, or epithets often cause racism and racial harassment to go underground or to surface in other, different forms.

Colleges and universities should initiate, develop, and implement programs and activities to educate students—indeed, the entire campus community—about tolerance for people with different racial, cultural, ethnic, and religious heritages. Orientation programs for entering students and ongoing seminars and forums on racial and gender issues, for example, would be appropriate beginnings for educating students when they first arrive on campus. Many institutions also are incorporating courses in their curricula, either required or elective, that focus on the history of racism and the civil rights movement in the United States, cultural diversity, gender, race, and religious prejudice, and the psychology and sociology of developing attitudes and values.

Either in the classroom or outside the formal class structure, the focus of educational programs and activities could be directed toward understanding the reasons for prejudice and bigotry and the development of sensitivity to and tolerance for other people and other cultures.

Students' Rights of Association and Assembly
Several guiding principles are appropriate for developing policy reconciling institutions' rights and responsibilities with their students' rights of association and assembly.

- Once some student groups have been recognized, or registered, by their institution, other groups should not be denied such treatment simply because the college or university does not agree with their views.
- Student groups should be given equal treatment, i.e., treated the same as other groups in the past have been treated, provided they fulfill the same established institutional procedural and substantive requirements.
- Colleges and universities are within their rights to emphasize, even through public statements, that their acknowledgment of the existence of student groups does not indicate institutional approval of the groups' or organizations' religious, political, economic, or philosophical positions.
- Students' freedom of association is no less protected by the U.S. Constitution when it advances religious views than when it advances other views.
- Demonstrations by students on public college campuses, like other associational activities, cannot be prohibited on the basis of content or the message to be communicated.
- Students' associational activities need not be tolerated if they infringe on the normal educational activities of the college or university or the rights of others; regulation of time, place, and manner is lawful for maintaining the institution's proper educational environment.
- Fraternities and sororities that are primarily social in nature and also part of a national organization may be treated, as a whole, differently from other student groups in terms of institutional recognition, including procedures and requirements for affiliation.
- Whatever an institution's relationship with its student Greek groups, that relationship should be conveyed to all applicable groups and their respective national organizations before institutional recognition or affiliation.

Thus, speech on the public college or university campus in the form of advocacy is protected by the Constitution; action, however, is not.

Thus, speech on the public college or university campus in the form of advocacy is protected by the Constitution; action, however, is not. Institutional administrators have a legitimate interest in preventing disruption of normal educational activities, but until physical disturbance or disruption occurs, they likewise hold a heavy burden to show their justification of any denial of free speech, a burden that courts have not taken lightly.

Benefits of recognizing student groups and student organizations allow those students to participate fully in the intellectual give and take of an institution of higher education whose espoused purpose is to promote educational growth and development in the marketplace of ideas.

Testing Athletes for Drugs

Many colleges and universities continue to be involved in disputes with their students, the NCAA, or both, over testing athletes for drugs. Reconciling the rights and responsibilities of higher education institutions while safeguarding the rights of student-athletes has been difficult, as the courts' rulings have shown. The numerous reversals and remands of athletes' cases indicate that judges remain undecided about the issues.

Perhaps the only nondebatable guideline available to institutional administrators is that, because of *NCAA* v. *Tarkanian* (1988), the implementation and enforcement of NCAA rules do not constitute state action, denoting, in effect, that students who object to mandatory drug testing will now register any legal claims in their respective institutions' state courts. While most issues regarding testing remain debatable, the courts are beginning to reach general consensus concerning the questions and principles they are addressing.

- Whether an institution chooses to go along with the NCAA's testing procedures or conduct its own testing program, it should develop clear and definitive policy objectives for its testing requirements and match its objectives to achieve the desired and stated outcome.
- Because the institution, if it participates in the NCAA's testing program, is the enforcer of any NCAA legislation against students, it could be subject to state laws and regulations relative to such enforcement and thus find itself between its students and the NCAA in legal claims brought by students.
- Courts have been unwilling in many instances to accept the NCAA's and colleges' and universities' stated purposes for drug testing.
- The accuracy of tests is limited, and procedural safeguards should be incorporated in drug testing programs to allow students who test positive to respond to or rebut the findings. Such students could be allowed access to an additional analysis by an independent laboratory.

- The courts' most recent rulings appear to support the position that institutional *mandatory* drug testing programs violate the principles of protection of privacy guaranteed in many state constitutions.
- Because of the protection of privacy, the courts are requiring colleges and universities to show a "compelling need" to test athletes, thereby treating them differently from other students.
- A strong consensus is evident among the courts that colleges and universities need to have drug education programs that emphasize prevention and rehabilitation, not only for athletes but for all students, and that such programs should hold high priority in terms of institutional support and visibility.

Colleges and universities best able to defend themselves and their drug testing programs to the courts have done so when they could document that their policies were designed for a significant, compelling reason, that the implementation of the policies accomplished their designed purpose, that the policies and their implementation specifically accommodate their respective state constitutional requirements of privacy and equal protection, and that they conform to requirements for due process in all matters, but particularly testing procedures, accuracy, and verification of test results.

Liability for Students' Safety
Students who sue colleges and universities for the harm to them resulting from violent crime or injuries sustained on campus generally claim that such harm is the result of the institution's negligence. To prove the college or university negligent, and therefore liable, students must first establish that their institution owed them a duty of care, that a breach of that duty caused them to suffer harm, and that the institution's conduct or lack thereof was the proximate cause of the harm that resulted in actual injury or loss. The necessary element for determining negligence is whether a duty of care exists.

Laws differ among the states, and courts likewise vary in their interpretations of the laws. General principles, however, resulting from adjudicated cases involving colleges and universities and their students, do exist for administrators relative to their concerns for students' safety and security on campus.

- Colleges and universities should show substantive efforts to warn students of foreseeable harm.
- Institutions generally are on notice of the potential for criminal harm if similar criminal incidents have occurred in the past; harm thus is foreseeable.
- Colleges and universities should show that they exercise reasonable care to keep the campus free from conditions that create or increase the risk of harm.
- If the college or university assumes a relationship of landowner or business and invitee with its students, it could be held to similar duties of private landlords in the maintenance of physical security on the premises.
- When higher education institutions have shown that their relationships with students are not sufficiently special (landlord/tenant, for example), the courts have been hesitant to impose upon them a duty to protect students from harm.
- When the college or university could not foresee harm to a student, the courts have been reluctant to impose liability on the institution for the harm.
- Courts generally have taken a hands-off position by rarely holding colleges liable for injuries to students resulting from the misuse or abuse of alcohol.
- Colleges and universities have best defended themselves before the courts from charges stemming from students' alcohol-related injuries by showing that they enforced state and local laws pertaining to the purchase and use of alcohol and that they provided educational programs to students and student groups concerning the use and abuse of alcohol.

Most personal injury cases brought by students against their colleges and universities to date have employed the concept of negligence in their arguments that the institution should be held liable for their injuries. In those cases, courts have used a common thread of analysis, ruling that a special relationship between the plaintiff student and the defendant college or university must be present to create a duty, the breach of which causes liability to attach.

The basic defenses against charges of institutional negligence are contributory negligence and assumption of risk. Contributory negligence has been used when the harm suffered could be partly or wholly attributed to the student's own negligence. Some states, however, allow for comparative negligence, attempting to prorate damages when contributory negligence has been shown.

Assumption of risk has been used when the institution could show that the injured student knew of the danger involved and voluntarily chose to accept the risk. In addition, public institutions in some states have used governmental immunity as a defense against negligence, but the concept has for the most part eroded during recent years. Charitable immunity, used in some states by privately supported colleges and universities as a defense against negligence, also has eroded, and the trend is toward treating charities like other business organizations.

A Final Word

This volume has presented a synthesis of the contemporary literature, including case law, pertaining to reconciling the rights and responsibilities of institutions of higher education and their students over issues of regulating offensive speech on campus, students' rights of association and assembly, mandatory drug testing of athletes, and liability regarding students' safety on campus. It presents implications of policy and practice for college and university administrators and faculty. The law evolves continuously, however, and anticipating specific changes or avoiding legal claims by students is not always possible. The most desirable institutional defense is to discern the educational, reasonable, and legal responsibilities appropriate for the institution and then design or modify policies and practices to meet those responsibilities. This volume should not be considered a substitute for the appropriate advice of legal counsel.

REFERENCES

The Educational Resources Information Center (ERIC) Clearinghouse on Higher Education abstracts and indexes the current literature on higher education for inclusion in ERIC's data base and announcement in ERIC's monthly bibliographic journal, *Resources in Education* (RIE). Most of these publications are available through the ERIC Document Reproduction Service (EDRS). For publications cited in this bibliography that are available from EDRS, ordering number and price code are included. Readers who wish to order a publication should write to the ERIC Document Reproduction Service, 7420 Fullerton Rd., Suite 110, Springfield, VA 22153-2852. (Phone orders with VISA or MasterCard are taken at 800-443-ERIC or 703-440-1400.) When ordering, please specify the document (ED) number. Documents are available as noted in microfiche (MF) and paper copy (PC). If you have the price code ready when you call EDRS, an exact price can be quoted. The last page of the latest issue of *Resources in Education* also has the current cost, listed by code.

Books and Periodicals

Alexandra, William Shaun. 1991. "Regulating Speech on Campus: A Plea for Tolerance." *Wake Forest Law Review* 26: 1349–87.

American Association of State Colleges and Universities. 1990. *How the First Amendment Applies to Offensive Expression on the Campuses of Public Colleges and Universities.* Washington, D.C.: Author.

American Association of University Professors. July/August 1992. "On Freedom of Expression and Campus Speech Codes." *Academe* 78: 30–31.

Bailey, Wilford S. 1991. *Achieving Integrity in Intercollegiate Athletics.* Occasional Paper No. 12. Washington, D.C.: Association of Governing Boards of Universities and Colleges.

Balkin, J.M. June 1990. "Some Realism about Pluralism: Legal Realist Approaches to the First Amendment." *Duke Law Journal:* 375–430.

Barr, Margaret J., and Associates, eds. 1988. *Student Services and the Law.* San Francisco: Jossey-Bass.

Bartlett, Katherine T., and Jean O'Barr. June 1990. "The Chilly Climate on College Campuses: An Expansion of the 'Hate Speech' Debate." *Duke Law Journal:* 574–86.

Baruch, Chad. 1990. "Dangerous Liaisons: Campus Racial Harassment Policies, the First Amendment, and the Efficacy of Suppression." *Whittier Law Review* 11: 697–721.

Battaglia, Jack M. 1991. "Regulation of Hate Speech by Educational Institutions: A Proposed Policy." *Santa Clara Law Review* 31: 345–85.

Bhirdo, Kelley W. Summer 1989. "The Liability and Responsibility of Institutions of Higher Education for the On-Campus Victimization of Students." *Journal of College and University Law* 16: 119–35.

Bok, Derek C. Winter 1985. "Reflections on Free Speech: An Open Letter to the Harvard Community." *Educational Record* 16: 4–9.

Brown, Valerie L. March 1990. "College Fraternities and Sororities: Tort Liability and the Regulatory Authority of Public Institutions of Higher Education." *West's Education Law Reporter* 58: 1–12.

———. 16 January 1992. "The Campus Security Act and Campus Law Enforcement." *Education Law Reporter* 70: 1055–67.

Brownstein, Alan E. Spring 1991a. "Hate Speech at Public Universities: The Search for an Enforcement Model." *Wayne Law Review* 37: 1451–68.

———. Winter 1991b. "Regulating Hate Speech at Public Universities: Are First Amendment Values Functionally Incompatible with Equal Protection Principles?" *Buffalo Law Review* 39: 1–52.

Byrne, J. Peter. February 1991. "Racial Insults and Free Speech within the University." *Georgetown Law Journal* 79: 399–443.

Carnegie Foundation for the Advancement of Teaching. 1990. *Campus Life: In Search of Community.* Princeton, N.J.: Author. ED 320 492. 157 pp. MF–01; PC–07.

Champion, Walter T., Jr. 1991. "The NCAA's Drug Testing Policies: Walking a Constitutional Tightrope?" *North Dakota Law Review* 67: 269–80.

Chronicle of Higher Education. 6 April 1988. "Georgetown Won't Appeal Ruling on Treatment of Homosexuals" 34: 1.

———. 29 January 1992a. "State Appeals Court Upholds Ban on Random Drug Testing at U. of Colorado" 38: A36.

———. 12 February 1992b. "Campus Codes That Ban Hate Speech Are Rarely Used to Penalize Students" 38: A35.

———. 11 March 1992c. "Faculty Members at Berkeley Offer Courses to Satisfy 'Diversity' Requirement" 38: A1.

Council for the Advancement of Standards for Student Services/ Development Programs. 1986. *CAS Standards and Guidelines for Student Services/Development Programs.* Washington, D.C.: Author. ED 303 757. 92 pp. MF–01; PC–04.

Covell, Kerrie S., and Annette Gibbs. 1989–90. "Drug Testing and the College Athlete." *Creighton Law Review* 23: 1–18.

D'Amato, Anthony. Winter 1991. "Harmful Speech and the Culture of Indeterminacy." *William and Mary Law Review* 32: 329–52.

Dangelo, Charles J. Spring 1990. "The Individual Worker and Drug Testing: Tort Actions for Defamation, Emotional Distress, and Invasion of Privacy." *Duquesne Law Review* 28: 545–59.

Delgado, Richard. Winter 1991. "Campus Antiracism Rules: Constitutional Narratives in Collision." *Northwestern University Law Review* 85: 343–87.

Dessayer, Kathryn Marie, and Arthur J. Burke. Spring 1991. "Leaving Them Speechless: A Critique of Speech Restrictions on Campus." *Harvard Journal of Law and Public Policy* 14: 565–82.

Dutile, Fernand N. 1988. "God and Gays at Georgetown: Observations on *Gay Rights Coalition of Georgetown University Law Center v. Georgetown University." Journal of College and University Law* 11(1): 1–20.

——. Fall 1990. "Higher Education and the Courts: 1989." *Journal of College and University Law* 17: 149–242.

——. Fall 1991. "The Law of Higher Education and the Courts: 1990." *Journal of College and University Law* 18: 163–275.

Ehrlich, Robert, and Joseph Scimecca. Summer 1991. "Offensive Speech on Campus: Punitive or Educational Solutions?" *Educational Record* 72: 26–29.

Evans, John M. Spring 1990. "The NCAA Drug Program: Out of Bounds but Still in Play." *Journal of Law and Education* 19: 161–91.

France, Steve. July 1990. "Hate Goes to College." *ABA Journal* 76: 44–50.

Gale, Mary Ellen. Winter 1991. "Reimagining the First Amendment: Racist Speech and Equal Liberty." *St. John's Law Review* 65: 119–85.

Gehring, Donald D. 1991. "Legal Issues in the Administration of Student Affairs." In *Administration and Leadership in Student Affairs,* edited by Theodore K. Miller and Roger B. Winston, Jr. Muncie, Ind.: Accelerated Development, Inc.

Gibbs, Annette. 1989a. "Colleges and Gay Student Organizations: Administrators' Prerogatives." *NACUBO Business Officer* 22(7): 34–38.

——. Winter 1989b. "Concerns Regarding Legal Liability for Student Safety." *Journal of College and University Student Housing* 19: 3–6.

——. Winter/Spring 1990. "The Continuing Apartheid Debate on College Campuses: Administrators' Managerial Prerogatives." *Journal for Higher Education Management* 5: 27–32.

——. Winter 1991. "Drug Testing and College Athletes: A Dilemma for Institutional Administration." *CUPA Journal* 42: 27–32.

Gibbs, Annette, and James J. Szablewicz. March 1988. "Colleges' New Liabilities: An Emerging New In Loco Parentis." *Journal of College Student Development* 29: 100–106.

Greenawalt, Kent. Winter 1990. "Insults and Epithets: Are They Protected Speech?" *Rutgers Law Review* 42: 287–307.

Gregory, Dennis E. 1985. "Alcohol Consumption by College Students and Related Liability Issues." *Journal of Law and Education* 14: 43–53.

Grey, Thomas C. Winter 1991. "Discriminatory Harassment and Free Speech." *Harvard Journal of Law and Public Policy* 14: 157–64.

Gunther, Gerald. 1990. "Speech That Harms: An Exchange. Freedom for the Thought We Hate." *Academe* 76: 10–14.

Haas, Kenneth. Winter 1990. "The Supreme Court Enters the 'Jar Wars': Drug Testing, Public Employees, and the Fourth Amendment." *Dickinson Law Review* 94: 305–71.

Harvey, James C. 1990. "Fraternities and the Constitution: University-Imposed Relationship Statements May Violate Student Associational Rights." *Journal of College and University Law* 17(1): 11–42.

Hauser, Gregory F. Fall 1990. "Social Fraternities at Public Institutions of Higher Education: Their Rights under the 1st and 14th Amendments." *Journal of Law and Education* 19(4): 433–66.

Hendrickson, Robert M. 1991. *The Colleges, Their Constituencies, and the Courts.* Topeka, Kans.: National Organization on Legal Problems of Education.

Hendrickson, Robert M., and Annette Gibbs. 1986. *The College, the Constitution, and the Consumer Student: Implications for Policy and Practice.* ASHE-ERIC Higher Education Report No. 7. Washington, D.C.: Association for the Study of Higher Education. ED 280 429. 108 pp. MF–01; PC–05.

Hodulik, Patricia B. Spring 1990. "Prohibiting Discriminatory Harassment by Regulating Student Speech: A Balancing of First Amendment and University Interests." *Journal of College and University Law* 16: 573–87.

———. 1991. "Racist Speech on Campus." *Wayne Law Review* 37: 1433–50.

Horton, Nancy S. Spring 1992. "Traditional Single-Sex Fraternities on College Campuses: Will They Survive the 1990s?" *Journal of College and University Law* 18: 419–82.

Hulshizer, Robin M. January 1991. "Securing Freedom from Harassment without Reducing Freedom of Speech: *Doe* v. *University of Michigan.*" *Iowa Law Journal* 76: 383–403.

Hyde, Henry J., and George M. Fishman. Spring 1991. "The Collegiate Speech Protection Act of 1991: A Response to the New Intolerance in the Academy." *Wayne Law Review* 37: 1469–1524.

Jackson, Brian. October 1991. "The Lingering Legacy of In Loco Parentis: An Historical Survey and Proposal for Reform." *Vanderbilt Law Review* 44: 1135–64.

Jahn, Karon L. 1990. "Rights at Odds: Free Speech and Competing Constitutional Claims." Paper presented at the 76th Annual Conference of the Speech Communication Association, Chicago, Illinois. ED 325 873. 15 pp. MF–01; PC–01.

Johnson, William J. January 1992. "Crime Report." *CASE Currents* 18: 30–34.

Johnston, F. Bruce, Jr. 1989. "The Concept of Foreseeability as It Relates to Personal Injury Litigation in College and University Residence Halls." Ed.D. dissertation, Western Michigan Univ.

Kaplin, W.A. 1985. *The Law of Higher Education.* 2d ed. San Francisco: Jossey-Bass.

Keeton, W.P., ed. 1984. *Prosser and Keeton on the Law of Torts.* 5th rev. ed. St. Paul: West Publishing.

Knapp, Charles Feeney. October 1990. "Drug Testing and the Student-Athlete: Meeting the Constitutional Challenge." *Iowa Law Review*

76: 107–38.

Laney, James T. 6 April 1990. "Why Tolerate Campus Bigots?" *New York Times*.

Lange, Ellen E. November 1990. "Racist Speech on Campus: A Title VII Solution to a First Amendment Problem." *Southern California Law Review* 64: 105–34.

Laramee, William A. Fall 1991. "Racism, Group Defamation, and Freedom of Speech on Campus." *NASPA Journal* 29: 55–62.

Lawrence, Charles R., III. 1990. "Speech That Harms: An Exchange. Acknowledging the Victims' Cry." *Academe* 76: 10–14.

Leeson, Todd A. Fall 1989. "The Drug Testing of College Athletes." *Journal of College and University Law* 16: 325–41.

McEvoy, Sharlene A. Spring 1992. "Campus Insecurity: Duty, Foreseeability, and Third Party Liability." *Journal of Law and Education* 21: 137–54.

McGee, Robert W. Fall 1990. "Hate Speech, Free Speech, and the University." *Akron Law Review* 24: 363–92.

McGowan, David F., and Ragesh K. Tangri. May 1991. "A Libertarian Critique of University Restrictions of Offensive Speech." *California Law Review* 79: 825–918.

McManus, Bill. Summer 1989. "*NCAA* v. *Tarkanian:* May a Student-Athlete Receive Constitutional Protection from the NCAA's Actions or Has the Final Door Been Closed?" *UMKC Law Review* 57: 949–62.

Maloney, Glenn W. 1988. "Student Organizations and Student Activities." In *Student Services and the Law,* edited by Margaret Barr. San Francisco: Jossey-Bass.

Massaro, Toni M. Winter 1991. "Equality and Freedom of Expression: The Hate Speech Dilemma." *William and Mary Law Review* 32: 211–66.

Matsuda, Mari J. August 1989. "Public Response to Racist Speech: Considering the Victim's Story." *Michigan Law Review* 87: 2320–81.

Meyer, Nancy J. March 1991. "Free Speech for College Students: How Much Is Enough?" *Communications and the Law* 13: 69–97.

Milani, Terrence E., and William R. Nettles III. Winter 1987. "Defining the Relationship between Fraternities and Sororities and the Host Institution." In *Fraternities and Sororities on the Contemporary College Campus,* edited by R.B. Winston, Jr., W.R. Nettles III, and J.H. Opper, Jr. New Directions for Student Services No. 40. San Francisco: Jossey-Bass.

Miyamoto, Tia. 1988. "Liabilities of Colleges and Universities for Injuries during Extracurricular Activities." *Journal of College and University Law* 15: 149–76.

Napier, Carol W. Fall 1991. "Can Universities Regulate Hate-Speech after *Doe* v. *University of Michigan?*" *Washington University Law Quarterly* 69: 991–98.

National Collegiate Athletic Association. 1991–92. *NCAA Drug Testing/ Education Programs, 1991–92*. Overland Park, Kans.: Author.

NCAA News. 21 October 1991. "Montana Judge Upholds Injunction Involving NCAA Testing Program" 28: 1+.

O'Neil, Robert M. 18 October 1989. "Colleges Should Seek Educational Alternatives to Rules That Override the Historic Guarantees of Free Speech." *Chronicle of Higher Education* 36: B1.

———. 1991a. "An Inquiry into the Legal and Ethical Problems of Campus Hate Speech." In *Free Speech Yearbook,* edited by Raymond S. Rodgers. Carbondale: Southern Illinois Univ. Press.

———. 18 December 1991b. "Point of View: Dealing with Intolerance for Intolerant Views." *Chronicle of Higher Education* 38: A44.

———. 8 July 1992. "A Time to Reevaluate Campus Speech Codes." *Chronicle of Higher Education* 38: A40.

Pernell, LeRoy. 1990. "Drug Testing of Student-Athletes: Some Contract and Tort Implications." *Denver University Law Review* 67: 279–300.

Post, Robert C. Winter 1991. "Racist Speech, Democracy, and the First Amendment." *William and Mary Law Review* 32: 267–328.

Ranney, James T. Winter 1990. "The Constitutionality of the Drug Testing of College Athletes: A Brandeis Brief for a Narrowly Intrusive Approach." *Journal of College and University Law* 16: 397–424.

Richmond, Douglas R. Summer 1990a. "Crime on Campus: When Is a University Liable?" *NASPA Journal* 27: 324–29.

———. Summer 1990b. "Institutional Liability for Student Organizations and Activities." *Journal of Law and Education* 19: 309–44.

Schaller, William L. Fall 1991. "Drug Testing and the Evolution of Federal and State Regulation of Intercollegiate Athletics: A Chill Wind Blows." *Journal of College and University Law* 18: 131–61.

Schmidt, Benno. Winter 1992. "The University and Freedom." *Academe* 73: 14–18.

Sedler, Robert A. Spring 1991. "*Doe* v. *University of Michigan* and Campus Bans on 'Racist Speech': The View from Within." *Wayne Law Review* 37: 1325–50.

SeLegue, Sean M. May 1991. "Campus Antislur Regulations: Speakers, Victims, and the First Amendment." *California Law Review* 79: 919–70.

Shapiro, John T. October 1990. "The Call for Campus Conduct Policies: Censorship or Constitutionally Permissible Limitations on Speech?" *Minnesota Law Review* 75: 201–38.

Sherry, Suzanna. February 1991. "Speaking of Virtue: A Republican Approach to University Regulation of Hate Speech." *Minnesota Law Review* 75: 933–44.

Siegel, Evan G.S. Fall 1990. "Closing the Campus Gates to Free Expression: The Regulation of Offensive Speech at Colleges and Universities." *Emory Law Journal* 39: 1351–1400.

Smith, Michael Clay. 1988. *Coping with Crime on Campus.* Washington, D.C.: ACE/Macmillan.

———. May 1990. "College Liability Resulting from Campus Crime: Resurrection for In Loco Parentis?" *West's Education Law Reporter* 59: 1–5.

Smolla, Rodney. Summer 1990. "Academic Freedom, Hate Speech, and the Idea of a University." *Law and Contemporary Problems* 53: 195–225.

Steinberg, Terry Nicole. Summer 1991. "Rape on College Campuses: Reform through Title IX." *Journal of College and University Law* 18: 39–65.

Stern, Kenneth S. 1990. *Bigotry on Campus: A Planned Response.* New York: American Jewish Committee, Institute of Human Relations. ED 328 108. 34 pp. MF–01; PC–02.

Stimpson, Catherine R. November/December 1991. "Meno's Boy: Hearing His Story—And His Sister's." *Academe* 77: 25–31.

Stone, Karen, and Judith R. Thompson. Spring 1989. "Drug Testing: A National Controversy." *Journal of Alcohol and Drug Education* 34: 70–79.

Strossen, Nadine. June 1990. "Regulating Racist Speech on Campus: A Modest Proposal?" *Duke Law Journal:* 484–573.

Teagarden, C. Claude. 25 April 1991. "Suspicionless Punitive Urinalysis Testing of College and University Student-Athletes." *Education Law Reporter* 65: 999–1020.

Thelin, John R., and Lawrence L. Wiseman. 1989. *The Old College Try: Balancing Academics and Athletics in Higher Education.* ASHE-ERIC Higher Education Report No. 4. Washington, D.C.: Association for the Study of Higher Education. ED 317 103. 158 pp. MF–01; PC–07.

Tricker, Raymond, and David L. Cook. Winter 1989. "The Current Status of Drug Intervention and Prevention in College Athletic Programs." *Journal of Alcohol and Drug Education* 34: 38–45.

U.S. General Accounting Office. 1989. *Drug Misuse: Anabolic Steroids and Human Growth Hormone.* Washington, D.C.: Author.

Watterson, Kim M. Summer 1991. "The Power of Words: The Power of Advocacy Challenging the Power of Hate Speech." *University of Pittsburgh Law Review* 52: 955–87.

Weinberg, Beverly. Spring 1991. "Treating the Symptom instead of the Cause: Regulating Student Speech at the University of Connecticut." *Connecticut Law Review* 23: 743–810.

Weinstein, James. Fall 1991. "A Constitutional Roadmap to the Regulation of Campus Hate Speech." *Wayne Law Review* 38: 163–247.

Cases and Statutes

American Bookseller Ass'n, Inc. v. *Hudnit,* 771 F.2d 323 (7th Cir. 1985).

Auburn Alliance for Peace and Justice v. *Martin,* 684 F. Supp. 1072 (M.D. Ala. 1988).

Bally v. *Northeastern University,* 403 Mass. 713 (1989), 532 N.E.2d 49 (Mass. 1989).

Beach v. *University of Utah,* 716 P.2d 413 (Utah 1986).

Berger v. *Battaglia,* 779 F.2d 992 (4th Cir. 1985), *cert. denied,* 476 U.S. 1159, 106 S.Ct. 2278 (1986).

Bradshaw v. *Rawlings,* 612 F.2d 135 (3d Cir. 1979), *cert. denied,* 446 U.S. 909 (1980).

Broadrick v. *Oklahoma,* 413 U.S. 601, 93 S.Ct. 2908 (1973).

Brown v. *North Carolina Wesleyan College,* 65 N.C. App. 579, 309 S.E.2d 701 (1983).

Chaplinsky v. *New Hampshire,* 315 U.S. 568, 62 S.Ct. 769 (1942).

Chess v. *Widmar,* 635 F.2d 1310 (8th Cir. 1980); *aff'd, Widmar* v. *Vincent,* 454 U.S. 263 (1981).

Clark v. *Community for Creative Non-Violence,* 468 U.S. 288 (1984).

Cohen v. *California,* 403 U.S. 15, 91 S.Ct. 1780 (1971).

Collin v. *Smith,* 578 F.2d 1197 (7th Cir. 1978).

D.C. Code 1-2520 (Washington, D.C. 1987).

Dercleyn v. *University of Colorado,* 832 P.2d 1031 (Colo. App. 1991).

District Board of Trustees of Miami Dade Community Colleges v. *M.H.,* 578 So. 2d 8 (D.C.A., Fla. 1991).

Dixon v. *Alabama State Board of Education,* 294 F.2d 150 (1961).

Doe v. *University of Michigan,* 721 F. Supp. 852 (E.D. Mich. 1989).

Furek v. *University of Delaware,* 594 A.2d 506 (Del. Sup. 1991).

Gay Activists Alliance v. *Board of Regents of University of Oklahoma,* 638 P.2d 1116 (Okla. 1981).

Gay Rights Coalition of Georgetown University Law Center v. *Georgetown University,* 536 A.2d 1 (D.C. 1987).

Gay Student Services v. *Texas A&M University,* 737 F.2d 1317 (5th Cir. 1984); *rehearing denied,* 105 S.Ct. 1860 (1985).

Healy v. *James,* 92 S.Ct. 2338 (1972).

Hegel v. *Langsam,* 273 N.E.2d 351 (Ohio Ct. of Common Pleas 1971).

Hill v. *NCAA,* No. 619209 (Cal. Super., Santa Clara County, Aug. 10, 1988); 273 Cal. Rptr. 402 (Cal. App. 6th Dist. 1990).

Houston v. *Hill,* 482 U.S. 451 (1987).

Iota Xi Chapter of Sigma Chi Fraternity v. *George Mason University,* 773 F. Supp. 792 (E.D. Va. 1991).

Levant and Hill v. *NCAA,* No. 619209 (Cal. Super., Santa Clara County, March 13, 1987).

McDonnell v. *Hunter,* 612 F. Supp. 1122 (S.D. Iowa 1984); *aff'd,* 746 F.2d 785 (8th Cir. 1984).

Miller v. *State of New York,* 466 N.Y.S.2d 436 (1983), 478 N.Y.S.2d 829 (Ct. App. 1984), 487 N.Y.S.2d 115 (1985).

Mullins v. *Pine Manor College*, 389 Mass. 47, 449 N.E.2d 331 (1983).

NAACP v. *Button*, 371 U.S. 415 (1963).

NCAA v. *Tarkanian*, 109 S.Ct. 454, 57 L.W. 4050 (1988).

O'Halloran v. *University of Washington*, 679 F. Supp. 997 (W.D. Wash. 1988); *rev'd*, 856 F.2d 1375 (9th Cir. 1988).

Peterson v. *San Francisco Community College District*, 685 P.2d 1131 (Cal. 1984).

Police Department of Chicago v. *Mosley*, 408 U.S. 92 (1972).

R.A.V. v. *St. Paul, Minn.*, 464 N.W.2d 507 (1991); 60 L.W. 4667 (June 23, 1992), *Slip. op.*

Relyea v. *State of Florida*, 385 So. 2d 1378 (Fla. App., 4th Dist. 1980).

Russell v. *Board of Regents of University of Nebraska*, 423 N.W.2d 126 (Neb. 1988).

Schaill by Kross v. *Tippecanoe County School Corporation*, 864 F.2d 1309 (7th Cir. 1988).

Skinner v. *Railway Labor Executives' Association*, 109 S.Ct. 1402 (1989).

Smith v. *Goguen*, 415 U.S. 556 (1974).

Spence v. *Washington*, 418 U.S. 405 (1974).

Street v. *New York*, 394 U.S. 576, 89 S.Ct. 1354 (1969).

Students Against Apartheid Coalition v. *O'Neil*, 660 F. Supp. 333 (W.D. Va. 1987a).

Students Against Apartheid Coalition v. *O'Neil*, 671 F. Supp. 1105 (W.D. Va. 1987b).

Students Against Apartheid Coalition v. *O'Neil*, 838 F.2d 735 (4th Cir. 1988).

Student Services for Lesbians/Gays v. *Texas Tech*, 635 F. Supp. 776 (N.D. Tex. 1986).

Tanja H. v. *Regents of the University of California*, 278 Cal. Rptr. 918 (Cal. App. 1 Dist. 1991).

Texas v. *Johnson*, 491 U.S. 397, 109 S.Ct. 2533 (1989).

Tinker v. *Des Moines Independent Community School District*, 393 U.S. 503 (1969).

University of California Regents v. *Bakke*, 438 U.S. 265, 98 S.Ct. 2733 (1978).

University of Utah Students Against Apartheid v. *Peterson*, 649 F. Supp. 1200 (D. Utah 1986).

UWM Post v. *Board of Regents of University of Wisconsin*, 774 F. Supp. 1163 (E.D. Wis. 1991).

Whitlock v. *University of Denver*, 712 P.2d 1072 (Colo. App. 1985), 744 P.2d 54 (Colo. 1987).

Widmar v. *Vincent*, 454 U.S. 263 (1981).

INDEX

A

Advocacy entitled to full protection, 34
Action not entitled to protection, 34
Alcohol-Related Injuries, 57-59
Association and Assembly Rights, 2
Auburn University, 32-33

B

Benefits of Recognition, 23-24
Brown University, 1

C

CAS Standards and Guidelines, 30
Central Connecticut State College, 23
Charitable immunity, 62
College Exposure to Liability, 3-4, 49-63
        concept of foreseeability, 4
        recommendations, 69-71
Conduct as protected speech, 32

D

Delaware Valley College, 57-58
Demonstrations, 30
Disruptive speech, 32-34
Drug education, 42-43
Drug testing program, see testing college athletes for drugs
Duty to adequately protect, 51-52

F

Federal Constitutional Jurisdiction, 40-41
Florida Atlantic University, 53

G

Gay/Lesbian Student Groups, 24-27
George Mason University, 1, 14-15
Georgetown University, 26-27
Governmental immunity, 62
Greek Organizations, 28-30

I

Immunity, see governmental or charitable immunity
Injuries to Students Not Involving Assaults, 54-57

L

Liability, see College Exposure to Liability

ASHE-ERIC HIGHER EDUCATION REPORTS

Since 1983, the Association for the Study of Higher Education (ASHE) and the Educational Resources Information Center (ERIC) Clearinghouse on Higher Education, a sponsored project of the School of Education and Human Development at The George Washington University, have cosponsored the *ASHE-ERIC Higher Education Report* series. The 1992 series is the twenty-first overall and the fourth to be published by the School of Education and Human Development at the George Washington University.

Each monograph is the definitive analysis of a tough higher education problem, based on thorough research of pertinent literature and institutional experiences. Topics are identified by a national survey. Noted practitioners and scholars are then commissioned to write the reports, with experts providing critical reviews of each manuscript before publication.

Eight monographs (10 before 1985) in the ASHE-ERIC Higher Education Report series are published each year and are available on individual and subscription bases. Subscription to eight issues is $90.00 annually; $70 to members of AAHE, AIR, or AERA; and $60 to ASHE members. All foreign subscribers must include an additional $10 per series year for postage.

To order single copies of existing reports, use the order form on the last page of this book. Regular prices, and special rates available to members of AAHE, AIR, AERA and ASHE, are as follows:

Series	Regular	Members
1990 to 92	$17.00	$12.75
1988 and 89	15.00	11.25
1985 to 87	10.00	7.50
1983 and 84	7.50	6.00
before 1983	6.50	5.00

Price includes book rate postage within the U.S. For foreign orders, please add $1.00 per book. Fast United Parcel Service available within the contiguous U.S. at $2.50 for each order under $50.00, and calculated at 5% of invoice total for orders $50.00 or above.

All orders under $45.00 must be prepaid. Make check payable to ASHE-ERIC. For Visa or MasterCard, include card number, expiration date and signature. A bulk discount of 10% is available on orders of 10 or more books, and 40% on orders of 25 or more books (not applicable on subscriptions).

Address order to
  ASHE-ERIC Higher Education Reports
  The George Washington University
  1 Dupont Circle, Suite 630
  Washington, DC 20036
Or phone (202) 296-2597
  Write or call for a complete catalog.

1992 ASHE-ERIC Higher Education Reports

1. The Leadership Compass: Values and Ethics in Higher Education
   John R. Wilcox and Susan L. Ebbs

2. Preparing for a Global Community: Achieving an International
   Perspective in Higher Education
   Sarah M. Pickert

3. Quality: Transforming Postsecondary Education
   Ellen Earle Chaffee and Lawrence A. Sherr

4. Faculty Job Satisfaction: Women and Minorities in Peril
   Martha Wingard Tack and Carol Logan Patitu

1991 ASHE-ERIC Higher Education Reports

1. Active Learning: Creating Excitement in the Classroom
   Charles C. Bonwell and James A. Eison

2. Realizing Gender Equality in Higher Education: The Need to
   Integrate Work/Family Issues
   Nancy Hensel

3. Academic Advising for Student Success: A System of Shared
   Responsibility
   Susan H. Frost

4. Cooperative Learning: Increasing College Faculty Instructional
   Productivity
   David W. Johnson, Roger T. Johnson, and Karl A. Smith

5. High School–College Partnerships: Conceptual Models, Programs, and Issues
   Arthur Richard Greenberg

6. Meeting the Mandate: Renewing the College and Departmental
   Curriculum
   William Toombs and William Tierney

7. Faculty Collaboration: Enhancing the Quality of Scholarship
   and Teaching
   Ann E. Austin and Roger G. Baldwin

8. Strategies and Consequences: Managing the Costs in Higher
   Education
   John S. Waggaman

1990 ASHE-ERIC Higher Education Reports

1. The Campus Green: Fund Raising in Higher Education
   Barbara E. Brittingham and Thomas R. Pezzullo

2. The Emeritus Professor: Old Rank - New Meaning
   James E. Mauch, Jack W. Birch, and Jack Matthews

3. "High Risk" Students in Higher Education: Future Trends
   Dionne J. Jones and Betty Collier Watson

4. Budgeting for Higher Education at the State Level: Enigma, Paradox, and Ritual
   Daniel T. Layzell and Jan W. Lyddon

5. Proprietary Schools: Programs, Policies, and Prospects
   John B. Lee and Jamie P. Merisotis

6. College Choice: Understanding Student Enrollment Behavior
   Michael B. Paulsen

7. Pursuing Diversity: Recruiting College Minority Students
   Barbara Astone and Elsa Nuñez-Wormack

8. Social Consciousness and Career Awareness: Emerging Link in Higher Education
   John S. Swift, Jr.

1989 ASHE-ERIC Higher Education Reports

1. Making Sense of Administrative Leadership: The 'L' Word in Higher Education
   Estela M. Bensimon, Anna Neumann, and Robert Birnbaum

2. Affirmative Rhetoric, Negative Action: African-American and Hispanic Faculty at Predominantly White Universities
   Valora Washington and William Harvey

3. Postsecondary Developmental Programs: A Traditional Agenda with New Imperatives
   Louise M. Tomlinson

4. The Old College Try: Balancing Athletics and Academics in Higher Education
   John R. Thelin and Lawrence L. Wiseman

5. The Challenge of Diversity: Involvement or Alienation in the Academy?
   Daryl G. Smith

6. Student Goals for College and Courses: A Missing Link in Assessing and Improving Academic Achievement
   Joan S. Stark, Kathleen M. Shaw, and Malcolm A. Lowther

7. The Student as Commuter: Developing a Comprehensive Institutional Response
   Barbara Jacoby

8. Renewing Civic Capacity: Preparing College Students for Service and Citizenship
   Suzanne W. Morse

1988 ASHE-ERIC Higher Education Reports

1. The Invisible Tapestry: Culture in American Colleges and Universities
   George D. Kuh and Elizabeth J. Whitt

2. Critical Thinking: Theory, Research, Practice, and Possibilities
Joanne Gainen Kurfiss

3. Developing Academic Programs: The Climate for Innovation
Daniel T. Seymour

4. Peer Teaching: To Teach is To Learn Twice
Neal A. Whitman

5. Higher Education and State Governments: Renewed Partnership, Cooperation, or Competition?
Edward R. Hines

6. Entrepreneurship and Higher Education: Lessons for Colleges, Universities, and Industry
James S. Fairweather

7. Planning for Microcomputers in Higher Education: Strategies for the Next Generation
Reynolds Ferrante, John Hayman, Mary Susan Carlson, and Harry Phillips

8. The Challenge for Research in Higher Education: Harmonizing Excellence and Utility
Alan W. Lindsay and Ruth T. Neumann

1987 ASHE-ERIC Higher Education Reports

1. Incentive Early Retirement Programs for Faculty: Innovative Responses to a Changing Environment
Jay L. Chronister and Thomas R. Kepple, Jr.

2. Working Effectively with Trustees: Building Cooperative Campus Leadership
Barbara E. Taylor

3. Formal Recognition of Employer-Sponsored Instruction: Conflict and Collegiality in Postsecondary Education
Nancy S. Nash and Elizabeth M. Hawthorne

4. Learning Styles: Implications for Improving Educational Practices
Charles S. Claxton and Patricia H. Murrell

5. Higher Education Leadership: Enhancing Skills through Professional Development Programs
Sharon A. McDade

6. Higher Education and the Public Trust: Improving Stature in Colleges and Universities
Richard L. Alfred and Julie Weissman

7. College Student Outcomes Assessment: A Talent Development Perspective
Maryann Jacobi, Alexander Astin, and Frank Ayala, Jr.

8. Opportunity from Strength: Strategic Planning Clarified with Case Examples
   Robert G. Cope

1986 ASHE-ERIC Higher Education Reports

1. Post-tenure Faculty Evaluation: Threat or Opportunity?
   Christine M. Licata

2. Blue Ribbon Commissions and Higher Education: Changing Academe from the Outside
   Janet R. Johnson and Laurence R. Marcus

3. Responsive Professional Education: Balancing Outcomes and Opportunities
   Joan S. Stark, Malcolm A. Lowther, and Bonnie M.K. Hagerty

4. Increasing Students' Learning: A Faculty Guide to Reducing Stress among Students
   Neal A. Whitman, David C. Spendlove, and Claire H. Clark

5. Student Financial Aid and Women: Equity Dilemma?
   Mary Moran

6. The Master's Degree: Tradition, Diversity, Innovation
   Judith S. Glazer

7. The College, the Constitution, and the Consumer Student: Implications for Policy and Practice
   Robert M. Hendrickson and Annette Gibbs

8. Selecting College and University Personnel: The Quest and the Question
   Richard A. Kaplowitz

1985 ASHE-ERIC Higher Education Reports

1. Flexibility in Academic Staffing: Effective Policies and Practices
   Kenneth P. Mortimer, Marque Bagshaw, and Andrew T. Masland

2. Associations in Action: The Washington, D.C. Higher Education Community
   Harland G. Bloland

3. And on the Seventh Day: Faculty Consulting and Supplemental Income
   Carol M. Boyer and Darrell R. Lewis

4. Faculty Research Performance: Lessons from the Sciences and Social Sciences
   John W. Creswell

5. Academic Program Review: Institutional Approaches, Expectations, and Controversies
   Clifton F. Conrad and Richard F. Wilson

6. Students in Urban Settings: Achieving the Baccalaureate Degree
   Richard C. Richardson, Jr. and Louis W. Bender

7. Serving More Than Students: A Critical Need for College Student Personnel Services
   Peter H. Garland

8. Faculty Participation in Decision Making: Necessity or Luxury?
   Carol E. Floyd

1984 ASHE-ERIC Higher Education Reports

1. Adult Learning: State Policies and Institutional Practices
   K. Patricia Cross and Anne-Marie McCartan

2. Student Stress: Effects and Solutions
   Neal A. Whitman, David C. Spendlove, and Claire H. Clark

3. Part-time Faulty: Higher Education at a Crossroads
   Judith M. Gappa

4. Sex Discrimination Law in Higher Education: The Lessons of the Past Decade. ED 252 169.*
   J. Ralph Lindgren, Patti T. Ota, Perry A. Zirkel, and Nan Van Gieson

5. Faculty Freedoms and Institutional Accountability: Interactions and Conflicts
   Steven G. Olswang and Barbara A. Lee

6. The High Technology Connection: Academic/Industrial Cooperation for Economic Growth
   Lynn G. Johnson

7. Employee Educational Programs: Implications for Industry and Higher Education. ED 258 501.*
   Suzanne W. Morse

8. Academic Libraries: The Changing Knowledge Centers of Colleges and Universities
   Barbara B. Moran

9. Futures Research and the Strategic Planning Process: Implications for Higher Education
   James L. Morrison, William L. Renfro, and Wayne I. Boucher

10. Faculty Workload: Research, Theory, and Interpretation
    Harold E. Yuker

*Out-of-print. Available through EDRS. Call 1-800-443-ERIC.

ORDER FORM

Quantity   **Amount**

_____ Please begin my subscription to the 1992 *ASHE-ERIC Higher Education Reports* at $90.00, 33% off the cover price, starting with Report 1, 1992.   _____

_____ Please send a complete set of the 1991 *ASHE-ERIC Higher Education Reports* at $80.00, 41% off the cover price.   _____

_____ Outside the U.S., add $10.00 per series for postage.   _____

Individual reports are avilable at the following prices:

1990 and 1991, $17.00	1983 and 1984, $7.50
1988 and 1989, $15.00	1982 and back, $6.50
1985 to 1987, $10.00	

Book rate postage within the U.S. is included. Outside U.S., please add $1.00 per book for postage. Fast U.P.S. shipping is available within the contiguous U.S. at $2.50 for each order under $50.00, and calculated at 5% of invoice total for orders $50.00 or above. All orders under $45.00 must be prepaid.

PLEASE SEND ME THE FOLLOWING REPORTS:

Quantity	Report No.	Year	Title	Amount

Please check one of the following:

☐ Check enclosed, payable to GWU–ERIC.
☐ Purchase order attached ($45.00 minimum).
☐ Charge my credit card indicated below:
  ☐ Visa   ☐ MasterCard

Subtotal: _____
Foreign or UPS: _____
Total Due: _____

Expiration Date _____

Name _____

Title _____

Institution _____

Address _____

City _____ State _____ Zip _____

Phone _____

Signature _____ Date _____

SEND ALL ORDERS TO:
ASHE-ERIC Higher Education Reports
The George Washington University
One Dupont Circle, Suite 630
Washington, DC 20036-1183
Phone: (202) 296-2597